SIX MYTHS

IN MODERN FINANCE THAT EVERY
INVESTOR NEEDS TO KNOW

RICHARD R. JOSS

CLASSIC DAY
PUBLISHING

Seattle, Washington
Portland, Oregon
Denver, Colorado
Vancouver, B.C.
Scottsdale, Arizona
Minneapolis, Minnesota

ISBN: 978-1-59849-068-8 (paperback)
ISBN: 978-1-59849-069-5 (hardback)

Printed in the United States of America

Illustrations: Lindsey Craft
Design: Soundview Design Studio

Classic Day Publishing
2925 Fairview Avenue East
Seattle, Washington 98102
877-728-8837
info@classicdaypub.com

TABLE OF CONTENTS

INTRODUCTION

The seeds for this book were sown back in 1992. At the time I was serving as the chief technical actuary for the employee benefits consulting firm of Watson Wyatt Worldwide, and I had been recently hired to serve as an expert witness in a court case involving actuarial assumptions. As part of the proceedings I learned of an investment forecasting model that was commonly taught at the nation's leading business schools. In spite of the acceptance of the formula by the academic finance community, it seemed to me as if it had a mathematical problem. Using mathematical language, the formula was treating raw data that was conditional in nature as if it could be treated as independent in nature. Conditional data is data where each new element is based in part on the data elements that preceded it in time. With independent data the prior history has no bearing any new piece of data.

This issue is purely a mathematical one. While the particular application that caught my attention came from the area of academic finance, the issue of whether raw data should be treated as conditional or independent data would be the same whether it arose from biology, political science, or any number of other possible sources. When conditional data is incorrectly treated as independent data, it skews the resulting analysis.

I retired from the actuarial profession in 2001 and was sufficiently curious about the conditional vs. independent issue in academic finance that I spent two years learning about mathematical applications in this arena. This research confirmed that the issue that bothered me in 1992 had not yet been fully addressed. The realization that the mathematics of conditional probabilities could play a very significant role in academic finance led me to write three technical papers on this topic.

These papers have all been published in the *Journal of Financial and Economic Practice* (JFEP). They are:

1) Correcting the Overstatement in Investment Forecasts – JFEP (Fall 2004);

2) The Tendency of the Arithmetic Mean to Overstate Expected Returns – JFEP (Fall 2005); and

3) Analyzing Investment Data Using Conditional Probabilities: The Implications for Investment Forecasts, Stock Option Pricing, Risk Premia, and CAPM Beta Calculations – JFEP (Spring 2006)

The reason for writing this book now is that 2008 has been a very tumultuous year in the stock market. The market itself has gone on a dramatic roller coaster ride, and several well-known financial institutions have gone out of business. Mainstream business publications such as *Business Week, Fortune*, and *The Economist* have all published articles that express concern about the reliability of some of the mathematical models of modern academic finance.

The very real concerns about the mathematics of academic finance presented in the three technical papers noted above are likely a contributing factor to the concerns identified by the mainstream business publications. However, to have technical analysis wind its way through the halls of academia is very time-consuming. This is especially true when the author of the technical analysis is not a member of the established academic finance community. Furthermore, since the papers confront some very long-held views of conventional wisdom in modern academic finance, the ideas presented are sure to meet with some natural resistance.

The goal of this book is to convert the technical concerns identified in the three published papers into easily-grasped illustrations. Given the sophisticated nature of the mathematics involved, this is not an easy task. However, if this task is successful, the mathematical problems of modern finance will become more visible to a wider audience, which will include general investors. If this happens, the changes needed in the mathematical models of modern finance will likely be made more quickly than if general investor participation is absent.

The material presented in *Six Myths in Modern Finance that Every Investor Needs to Know* is organized as follows:

Chapter 1 provides necessary background information and lays out the process that will be used to demonstrate that several key conclusions of modern finance are simply not true. It is one thing to demonstrate a key conclusion is not true, and it is another to provide the reason for the inaccuracy. It is the goal of this book to provide both the demonstration and the reason.

Chapter 2 gives a more complete description of the data that is used for illustration purposes throughout the remainder of the book. In some ways it is easier to demonstrate a problem using hypothetical data, but that would leave the demonstration open to challenge. Thus, all the key demonstrations in this book will be done with data that was specifically selected to reflect actual market behavior.

Chapters 3, 4, and 5 cover three myths in modern finance dealing with general investment forecasting and the conditional nature of historical investment return data. In each case the development of the demonstration is described in detail. The specific final demonstration is most commonly a chart or a graph that shows that the conclusion of modern finance that is under consideration cannot possibly be true. In addition, since each of the myths that are being exposed has a direct impact on investors, these impacts will be specifically highlighted once the demonstration is complete.

Chapter 6 is a brief primer on stock options and other derivative securities. This chapter is placed here because the three chapters that follow it all deal with myths concerning the pricing of stock options, and some of the readers of this book may not be familiar with this particular type of security. This chapter, and the three that follow, may be relevant to you, even if you do not purchase stock options on the open market. The myths in the three chapters that follow Chapter 6 are as relevant for employee stock options, a common employee compensation technique that has been cut back lately, as they are for general stock options that are traded on the open market. Perhaps when the myths concerning the pricing of stock options are exposed, the recently cut employee stock option programs may be restored.

Chapters 7, 8, and 9 cover three myths dealing with the pricing of stock options or a very well-known stock option pricing model: the Black-Scholes model. As you might expect, these concepts are highly mathematical. Thus, the demonstrations in these three chapters may involve more complex illustration than the demonstrations in Chapters 3, 4, and 5. But the issues are very important, and wider understanding of these concepts will be of benefit to all investors in the future.

Chapter 10 contains a few final comments.

This book is designed for general investors. I hope you find the exposed myths to be of interest and that the insights provided by the illustrations will open your eyes to the mathematical techniques and problems that are present in modern finance. These issues are very real and very important. The year 2008 has been a disastrous one for the financial services industry. Congress even appropriated a $700 billion bailout to help the financial services industry weather the current storm.

To the extent that purely mathematical problems have contributed to the difficulties faced by investment banks and other firms, they need to be addressed. $700 billion is a lot of money, averaging about $2,000 for every resident of the United States. For this level of expenditure, the taxpayers should at least expect that the mathematical issues that contribute to the problems in the financial services industry be corrected.

Richard R. Joss
Bellingham, WA
November 2008

Galileo Busts Aristotle's Myth

Chapter 1

BACKGROUND

It was in ancient Pisa, Galileo gained his fame.

A simple busted myth helped all to know his name.

As the two balls fell,

the crowd did swell.

Ari's age old myth was quickly put to shame.

MYTH BUSTING

Six Myths in Modern Finance that Every Investor Needs to Know is not so much about myths, as it is about myth busting. A myth is a commonly accepted understanding of conventional wisdom. Myth busting is the act of showing that this commonly accepted conventional wisdom is, in fact, not true. Myths may be busted by the mere passage of time and the emergence of new information. However, some myths have been busted by the use of a dramatic demonstration. It is the goal of this book to bust six myths in modern finance by the use of dramatic demonstration – showing conclusively that each of these commonly held bits of conventional wisdom cannot possibly be true.

Myth busting by dramatic demonstration has become popular in recent years. There is a television show devoted to debunking strange and unusual myths, and the Internet has many interesting videos of myth busting experiments. One humorous video in particular shows the interaction between diet soda and a popular candy. The video seems to be a bit of myth itself – but at least it is very entertaining. Google "myth busting," and you will find more examples of very entertaining videos all purporting to demonstrate scientifically that some particular commonly held belief is not true. While at times the science may seem a bit sketchy, at least the people doing the demonstrations are almost always wearing white scientific-looking lab coats and eye protection.

Although it is now an active part of our current culture, myth busting by demonstration has been around for centuries. Perhaps one of the greatest myth busting demonstrations of all time (at least according to myth) occurred in the late 1500's when Galileo climbed the steps of the Leaning Tower of Pisa. At the time he was a professor of mathematics at the University of Pisa, and the purpose of the climb was simply to drop two objects from the top of the tower. One of the objects was relatively light in weight, and the other relatively heavy. Galileo was in the process of a myth busting exercise. The only thing missing was the television cameras to record the entire event for posterity.

When Galileo made his famous climb, conventional wisdom held that the heavier object would fall faster that the lighter one, and would therefore hit the ground first. This particular bit of conventional wisdom had been in place since the time of Aristotle, who lived from 384 B.C. to 322 B.C. Thus, the myth that heavier objects fall faster than lighter ones had been in existence for almost 2,000 years! A crowd of students, professors, and priests watched the demonstration, and when both objects went "thud" at the same time, the myth was busted. Or so you might think.

According to another myth there is a little known sequel to the Galileo story. Three days after Galileo's experiment a leading scientist of the day, Ostrichini, climbed the Leaning Tower of Pisa carrying a cannon ball and a feather pillow. Of course, when Ostrichini threw both objects from the top of the tower, the cannon ball landed first; the feather pillow encountering significant wind resistance as it wafted its way back to earth. Ostrichini then ran through the streets of Pisa denouncing Galileo's experiment as a fake.

Actually, the followers of Aristotle were quite opposed to Galileo's new theory, notwithstanding his famous demonstration, and Galileo was forced to leave the University of Pisa because of his views. It seems that leading scientists of that day did not like to have their 2,000-year-old myth busted. They fought rather hard to hold on to their cherished belief, even in the face of compelling evidence to the contrary.

Another ancient example of myth busting by demonstration occurred in 1492 when Christopher Columbus sailed from Palos, Spain, to India. At least he thought it was India at the time he made his trip. The myth that was busted was the common belief that the world was flat. After all, if you find yourself standing in the middle of a Kansas corn field, the world sure does seem flat. Common sense would tell you this "flat earth" assumption must be true. But the Columbus voyage to India by sailing west instead of east, showed that the earth was, in fact, not flat, but round.

The exploits of Christopher Columbus show another side of myth busting. Myth busting exercises have the potential to be very dangerous. Certainly Columbus took a huge risk by sailing west to reach the East. He could have run afoul of a large Atlantic storm, never to be heard from again. Of course, then there would be more than just a few people left back on shore who knew the truth: he simply sailed off the edge of the world.

Actually, Christopher Columbus deserves another special mention in the Myth Busting Hall of Fame. His famous voyage showed that it was possible to miss your target by more than 10,000 miles and still have a successful myth-busting demonstration! When engaged in the practice of busting myths, one need not necessarily be 100% right in order to make one's point.

It would seem that myths could also be busted by detailed scientific calculations. Certainly this technique has been successful on numerous occasions, but it also has run into problems. Perhaps the best example of the difficulties of detailed scientific calculations is illustrated by the story of Nicholas Copernicus (1473-1543).

In Copernicus' time it was common to accept the 1,400-year-old myth of Ptolemy that the earth was the center of our solar system. Under this theory, known as the geocentric model of the solar system, the sun, the other planets, and the moon all revolved around the earth.

However, Copernicus doubted this theory. He felt that the sun was the center of the solar system and that the earth and other planets revolved around the sun. This is the model that is now referred to as the heliocentric model of the solar system. He laid out very detailed calculations in his magnificent book, *Concerning the Revolutions of Celestial Spheres*. In spite of the strength of his arguments, it took over 100 years for his ideas to become more fully embraced. After all, it is glaringly obvious that the sun rises in the east and sets in the west. The earth sits still and the sun goes around the earth. Or so it would seem.

As shown above, myth busting has quite a history. And as new theories are tried and tested, myth busting will stay in force as a means of debunking the false theories or, if the myth busting experiment fails, adding some measure of credibility to the theory. In short, it seems as if myth busting will be with us for a long, long time.

THE IMPACT OF MYTH BUSTING

At first thought, it seems rather surprising that the myth that heavier objects fall more rapidly than lighter ones went unchallenged for almost 2,000 years. But upon greater reflection, maybe it is not so surprising after all. The laws of gravity were the same laws before Galileo's famous experiment that they were after the experiment.

People still found it easier to walk down a flight of stairs than to walk up it. If you dropped a hammer, it still would manage to hit your toe. Ouch! Before Galileo's tower climb, people were able to go about their daily lives in spite of the incorrect common knowledge that heavier things fall faster than lighter ones. In short, the myth had very little impact on the lives of everyday folk before it was busted, and the correction of the myth had very little impact on the lives of everyday folk after it was corrected.

The same cannot be said for Christopher Columbus' voyage to the New World. The busting of the flat earth myth verified that the world was round. Prior to Columbus' great adventure, explorers tended to stay relatively close to shore, as they did not want to sail off the edge of the world. Christopher Columbus' trip started an era of global exploration that dramatically changed how the world functioned. In just over one century after Columbus' trip, European settlers began to take up residence in the Americas. This new development not only changed their lives dramatically, but the lives of the indigenous people of the New World. Columbus' 10,000 mile error had one other interesting consequence. Because of his error, the indigenous people of the New World have ever since been referred to as "Indians."

To put this development in perspective, it has now been nearly 40 years since man first set foot on the moon. But the chance of any moon colonies developing within the next 60 years seems very, very small. Thus, the Columbus myth-busting expedition had a very dramatic impact on people's lives. Perhaps the impact was not immediate, but significant life changes for some people occurred within a comparatively short time.

All of the myths that are the subject of this book come from the field of modern finance. These myths are conclusions reached in modern finance that this book will demonstrate are, in fact, not true. These myths do have a very real impact on investors. Decisions made by investors like you as to how much money to invest in stocks, or whether or not to invest in stocks at all, may have been based on some of the erroneous conclusions of modern finance. Had these investors been provided with correct information, the investment decisions may well have been different.

Over the past two decades it has been common for some companies to use employee stock option grants as part of the compensation package. Companies that have used employee stock options could also be affected by the myths covered in this book. Over the past two years many corporate employee stock option programs have been reduced dramatically, in part because of conclusions reached in modern finance. When these conclusions are shown to be false, perhaps these employee stock option programs can be returned to former levels.

In short, the myths that are busted in this book will have an impact, a very immediate impact, on the lives of people. The myths and the myth busting demonstrations in *Six Myths in Modern Finance that Every Investor Needs to Know* need to be studied and fully understood. The changes in modern finance that need to be made because of the demonstrations in this book are better made sooner rather than later.

MODERN FINANCE

Modern finance is the term often used to describe the application of the mathematical techniques of probability and statistics to help investors make reasonable and appropriate investment decisions. While modern finance has its detractors, the techniques have been around for about 50 years, and it appears clear that modern finance is now here to stay.

Furthermore, the techniques of modern finance are becoming available to more and more regular investors, not just those who manage large portfolios of assets. This book is designed to help these regular investors (as well as those who manage large portfolios) see some of the pitfalls of modern finance and the negative impact that these pitfalls may have on their investment decisions.

You are likely already aware of some of the conclusions of modern finance. For example, it is commonly accepted that over the long run, an investor will tend to earn more money by investing in stock investments than by investing in bonds. It is also commonly accepted that over the long run, an investor will tend to earn more money by investing in bonds than by buying certificates of deposit.

In each of the above illustrations, the commonly accepted theory is based on what has happened in the past. When one looks at an 80-year investment history, it is true that on average stock investments have done better than bond investments, and in turn, bond investments have had higher rates of return than certificates of deposit. The general reasoning has always been tied to risk. Stocks have been deemed to be riskier than bonds, because they tend to be more volatile than bonds – the value of a particular stock tends to go up and down further and more rapidly than the value of a particular bond. This volatility, the tendency to go up and down in value, is deemed to make the investment in stocks riskier than the investment in bonds. The reasoning then continues that for investors to take on this extra risk, they should be compensated with a higher rate of return. In the same line of reasoning, bonds have been deemed to be riskier than certificates of deposit, because they tend to be the more volatile of the two securities. The same theory then notes that bonds should have a higher overall rate of return than certificates of deposit to compensate investors for taking on the extra risk. But just because this pattern has happened in the past does not necessarily mean that it will happen in the future.

The fact that stock investments might not outperform bond investments in the short run has recently become painfully evident to many stock investors. At the time this book is being written, fall 2008, the stock market is taking a huge beating. In some cases stock portfolios may be worth only 60% of what they were a year earlier. For the first ten months of 2008, an investor would have been better off stuffing his or her money in a mattress than investing in stocks.

Because of the fact that stocks go up and down in value, modern finance attempts to quantify this dynamic of changing stock value in order to provide investors with more information than just the average return of 10%. Modern finance actually tries to calculate the probability of various investment outcomes. For example, you might see an article that says that there is a 20% chance that your stock investments will earn more than 25% for a given year. Or on the cautionary side, the same article might say that there is a 30% chance that your stock investments will actually go down in value for the year.

The article is providing the "percentage chance" information to help you make decisions about your investments, in much the same way that the TV weather person is using "percentage chance" of rain information to help you make decisions about your day. If there is a 90% chance of rain, you will probably want to carry your umbrella. What the 90% chance of rain means is that based on the weather models, satellite pictures, and all the sophisticated weather technology, if the same combination of atmospheric conditions existed for 10 days, the weather people would expect rain on 9 of those days, and no rain on only one day.

In the same vein, when the modern finance people tell you that there is a 20% chance that your investments will earn more than 25% for a given year, they are saying that based on their sophisticated models, if these same conditions existed for 10 years, the modern finance people would expect that for two of those years, you would earn at least the 25% investment return rate, but that for eight of them you would not. Whereas the 90% chance of rain information made the umbrella carrying decision easy, the 20% chance of a possible investment return does not yield an easy answer to the question: How should I invest my money for this year? It is information, however, and many investors in conjunction with their advisors will use this information to set up an investment portfolio that seems to be right for them.

The conclusions reached by modern finance are often combined with other non-investment related factors that might impact the right investment strategy for you. Other non-investment related factors include such items as: how old you are, whether you are investing for the long-term or short-term, and in general how tolerant you are of risk. Most investment advisors now have computer models that can help guide you into making an investment decision that seems to be best for you based on these and other factors.

Modern finance has become highly sophisticated, and the models in use today rely on lots of variables, not just history, in providing detailed information for investors to consider as they make critical investment decisions. The models not only guide average investors, but provide critical risk assessment guidance for people interested in sophisticated investments that have funny sounding names like credit default swaps. Modern finance has become a huge business. But as shown in this book modern finance has some mathematical problems, and they really need to be corrected.

MY INTRODUCTION TO MODERN FINANCE

I first learned of modern finance when I served as an expert witness for the law firm of Vinson & Elkins in the landmark 1992 Tax Court case, *Vinson & Elkins v. IRS*. A particular part of the case involved the appropriate selection of expected stock market returns. While I offered a very specific answer for an expected stock market return, the expert witness for the Internal Revenue Service (IRS) offered a stock market forecasting formula, which had a whole range of possible answers. The range of possible answers was based on the concept that stock market returns could be treated as if they were like the lottery drawings that one might see on television.

To put some visual imagery on this concept, imagine a giant rotating bin full of little balls, each one with a stock market return rate written on it. A certified representative of a major accounting firm walks up to the bin and proceeds to draw four balls. The first one has a 25% written on it, the second -2%, the third 18%, and the fourth one has 7% written on it. Add these four numbers together, divide by four, and you have calculated the average stock market return. In this illustration the number is 12%.

So far, this all seemed pretty straight forward. However, instead of just adding up the four numbers and dividing by four, the model used by the expert witness for the IRS had a specific formula for determining what the expected value of taking this average would be. This formula depended upon the number of balls taken out of the giant bin. Along with the formula came an interesting explanation. The explanation stated that due to a "statistical artifact," the calculated average stock market return (the number you would get by adding the numbers on the balls and dividing by the number of balls, i.e., the 12% number above) would tend to decrease as the number of balls drawn out of the bin increases. It was this explanation that caught my attention.

Continuing with the visual imagery, according to the formula presented by the expert witness for the IRS, if the certified representative of the major accounting firm continued to draw balls and then take the average, the average would be expected to decrease. Thus, if he or she were to draw 20 balls, add up the 20 numbers, and then divide by 20, the resulting average was expected to be something less than the original 12%, perhaps a number like 11%. If the certified representative continued to draw more balls, the forecasting formula presented by the expert witness indicated that the expected average return would continue to fall. By the time he or she reached 40 balls, added the numbers on the 40 balls, and divided this total by 40, the average was expected to reduce even further, to perhaps 10%. This was a most unusual giant rotating bin!

As a mathematician, I knew that there were no (repeat, NO) such rotating bins. The mathematical theory would say that the expected average for each set of drawn balls should be the same whether it was a set of 4 balls, 20 balls, or 40 balls. It did not matter what interpretation was provided for each number written on a ball, the expected average would not change with the number of balls drawn. The numbers on the balls could be stock market returns, or they could be the high temperature for October 7 in Seattle. The expected averages should not have been assumed to decrease as more balls are drawn out of the bin. Even though the formula was attributed to the Nobel-prize winning work of William F. Sharpe, something was not right, mathematically, with the formula.

I retired from the actuarial profession in 2001 and out of curiosity decided to see what had happened to the forecasting formula that had given me so much concern back in 1992. I was surprised to find that although the formula had been attributed to a Nobel Prize winner, it has now been removed from finance textbooks. The inaccuracy of the formula was also independently confirmed for me by a finance professor. Nobel Prize winners can and do make mistakes. We all do.

ROTATING BINS VS. ACTUAL MARKETS

While I was glad to see that the problem with the specific forecasting formula had been corrected, I was disappointed to see that the incorrect reasoning that was the source of the problem with the forecasting formula had not been addressed. This incorrect reasoning has to do with a basic mathematical difference between rotating bins and actual stock markets. While this difference may seem minor, the impact of this difference can actually be quite significant.

In the model presented by the expert witness for the IRS, the numbers that were written on the balls were just the observed investment returns from historical data. For example, if stocks had returned 28% for 1982, then 28% would be one of the numbers written on one of the balls. If stocks had returned -9% for 1987, then -9% would have been another number written on a different ball. On the surface, this seems pretty straight forward.

However, keep in mind that while standing in a Kansas corn field, the conclusion that the earth is flat seems pretty straight forward as well. Also, watching the sun rise in the east and set in the west day after day leads to a very reasonable conclusion that the sun rotates around the earth. Sometimes things that may seem reasonable at first glance turn out to be a bit more complicated. It is the contention of this book that writing each calendar year's return on a little ball, putting the collection of balls into a giant rotating bin, and then claiming investment return forecasting is comparable to drawing balls out of this bin is one of those times.

As noted above, the problem has to do with the difference between rotating bins and actual markets. To illustrate this problem, assume that for three years in a row actual stock markets have done pretty well. They returned 20% for one year, 18% for the second, and 27% for the third. The market has had a pretty good run! Continuing the illustration, assume that someone has a giant rotating bin, and that the first three numbers drawn out of the bin happen to be these exact same three numbers: 20, 18, and 27.

Now consider the dynamics that will affect the next, or fourth, number. In the case of the giant rotating bin, the fact that the three previous numbers were 20, 18, and 27 has no bearing whatsoever on the outcome of the next drawing. The next number could be relatively large, or it could be relatively small. All of the various numbers in the giant rotating bin have an equal chance of being drawn.

However, in the case of actual markets, articles in the financial press may begin to talk about market bubbles or irrational exuberance, that the market has become over-priced, that investors might consider some profit taking, and that price/earnings ratios are now higher than historical averages. All of these real market forces do have an impact. While there is still the potential for another great year in the stock market, there is subtle pressure for what has been commonly called a "market correction" or a year with a negative return (or at least a positive return that is not as large as the three years shown above) after a string of several years with large positive returns.

To continue with some visual imagery, it is as if the market is still somewhat like the giant rotating bin, but the balls with the negative numbers have become somewhat larger – making them more likely to be drawn; and the balls with the large positive numbers have become somewhat smaller – making them less likely to be drawn. All the balls are still in the giant rotating bin, and any particular ball still has the potential to be selected. But the market forces tend to tilt the exercise a bit toward not having another large positive year.

The same dynamic would occur following recent losses in the stock market. The financial press might feature articles about the market bottoming out, that price/earnings ratios are at historic lows, and that blue chip stocks seem to be offering a great value. All of these market forces would tend to make the negative numbered balls in the giant bin seem a bit smaller and less likely to be drawn, whereas the positive balls seem to become somewhat larger and more likely to be drawn.

Using technical language, the modern finance rotating bin model is treating historical investment return data as independently determined (random) events for statistical analysis purposes. But if one thinks about it for a while, it is quite clear that investment return rates are determined by changes in share value, and these changes in share value are made by actual investors who decides to either bid up or bid down a particular share price. The modern finance rotating bin model is based on the assumption that these investors pay no attention to recent market history before making the decision to buy or sell shares at a given price. The rotating bin model takes no account of such factors as market corrections, the impact of price/earnings ratios, or any other commonly accepted market impacts.

As a mathematician, it seemed to me that historical investment return data should have been treated as what are known as conditional (non-random) events. Each day's, week's or month's result is conditioned to some degree on the results that preceded it. If the preceding periods have had rates of return that have been better than average, then there is a subtle "push" to make the current period return lower than average. If the preceding periods have had rates of return that have been worse than average, then there is a subtle "push" to make the current period return better than average.

Using the mathematics appropriate for conditional events it is possible to create giant rotating bins in which the balls actually do get larger or smaller depending upon recent history. These next generation rotating bins significantly improve the forecasting capabilities of the basic rotating bin model. While the above language attempts to provide a certain visual imagery, the basic mathematical concept is quite technical. The goal of this book is to translate this technical concept into much more visible and understandable terms.

Many non-mathematicians may not appreciate the distinction between "independently determined events" and "conditional events." In fact, to some people those particular words may not mean anything at all. Even those who do understand the difference between independently determined events and conditional events may think that the distinction is probably not worth worrying about.

While this difference may seem minor to a non-mathematician and may even be minor in lots of cases, the impact in this particular case is actually quite large. When conditional data is treated as independent data in modern finance applications, the resulting formulas tend to overstate the expected gain and understate the expected risk. This is not a pretty combination of possible results.

MYTH BUSTING IN MODERN FINANCE

The three papers mentioned in the Introduction are all very mathematical in nature. They document some serious basic mathematical problems in modern finance. The goal of *Six Myths in Modern Finance that Every Investor Needs to Know* is to bring the key ideas included in the technical papers to the investing public through the use of dramatic illustration. Myth busting!

I am certainly not the first person to raise concerns about modern finance. Modern finance has had its detractors throughout its entire existence. One of the most well-known detractors is Nassim Nicholas Taleb, whose best-selling book *The Black Swan* highlights a valid concern with modern finance. Even when the giant rotating bin has been modified to reflect conditional events, the stock market is not a giant rotating bin, and the actual decisions made by investors that drive stock market performance are not the same as flipping coins, rolling dice, or drawing numbers out of a bin. Actual investors, the ones who really determine eventual stock market rates of return, are influenced by wars, personal circumstances, fear, hope, and whole range of other factors that cannot ever be fully captured by the mathematical techniques of probability and statistics.

In this regard it is not entirely unreasonable to consider the entire field of modern finance as a myth that needs busting. In terms of making dramatic demonstrations leading exactly to this point, Taleb does an excellent job. He documents well the case that some very significant, yet highly improbable events – called black swans by Taleb – can and do occur, and they may have a dramatic impact on an investor. And this dramatic impact occurs outside the accepted models of modern finance.

Modern finance appears as if it might be better suited to considering the risk characteristics of longer-term investments, where the ups and downs of market fortunes, perhaps even "positive" and "negative" black swans (unpredictable events), have some time to balance each other out. If you go to Las Vegas and play a slot machine once, you could win or you could lose. But few people play just once! And the people in Las Vegas who set up the slot machine know that if you keep playing, the law of averages will eventually catch up to you. In this case the law of averages says that the casinos will earn their anticipated take of all the money gambled. The vast majority of recreational gamblers who go to Las Vegas leave some of their hard-earned money in town.

The same concept is what drives the theory of modern finance. Next year's stock return might be good or it might be bad, but if you keep playing the stock market, like someone playing a slot machine in Las Vegas, eventually the law of averages will catch up to you. But in this case, instead of leaving as a loser, your stock investments should work their way back to the point where they provide you with the relatively high long-term average return that has been seen historically. Or at least that is the theory.

While some detractors would like to treat the entire field of modern finance as a possible myth, this book takes a very different approach. This book accepts the premise that mathematical analysis of probability and statistics can help in the process of making investment decisions. But it advocates that the mathematics of conditional events should play a much larger role in this process than it has so far. It is the advocacy for this concept that is presented in the three technical papers.

However, as noted above in the case of Nicholas Copernicus, writing a detailed scientific document is not necessarily sufficient to overturn a deeply held myth. History has shown that it is far more likely that a myth can be busted if it is exposed as being false with a dramatic, irrefutable demonstration. But even here, myth busting is extremely difficult. Even though Galileo's experiment seemed to be completely fool proof, he was forced out of his position at the University of Pisa for his "unconventional" views. Myth busting can be a very difficult exercise!

EVERYDAY INVESTORS

Modern finance is beginning to play a role in the lives of everyday investors, not just professional money managers. For example, it is becoming more and more common for employers to provide investment planning assistance to employee participants in 401(k) or other savings plans. Sometimes this assistance includes a forecast of expected account balances at retirement under different investment scenarios.

Often employees will have access to a computer program where they may enter their actual account balances and see projections of what the accounts may be worth at retirement. Instead of showing just a single number, the projections are likely to show a range of possible results. There is a small probability that the markets will do very well, and you will become quite rich. There is also a small probability that the markets will do poorly and your account will not grow much at all. Somewhere in the middle is an "expected" account value.

By changing your future investment mix, the specific projections will change. For example, moving to a more conservative strategy (fewer stocks, more bonds), the small probability "quite rich" number will drop, but the small probability "not grow much" number will increase. This narrower gap might provide you with greater assurance that you will actually receive the "expected" account value.

These projections are an example of modern finance in action. They provide the employees with useful information, but the ultimate investment decision still rests with the employee and his or her advisors. One thing that is not commonly considered is: How reliable are the projections? Employees who use these programs are likely seeing vastly different projections in November 2008 than they saw in November 2007. The recent large drop in the stock market has provided a large, somewhat unanticipated, drop in the typical employee's 401(k) account balance.

While most investors are vaguely aware that the range of possible investment outcomes is based on history, they are probably not aware of the critical assumptions that drive the process. It is the goal of this book to highlight six critical areas of mathematical concern in modern finance. Once these areas are fully understood, an average investor will be likely to think twice about the decision he or she is about to make based on the forecasts developed using modern finance models. An awareness of the assumptions that drive the models, and an understanding of some of the unusual outcomes, will make the investor a better and wiser user of the techniques of modern finance.

All of the issues presented in *Six Myths in Modern Finance that Every Investor Needs to Know* are based on the mathematics of modern finance and do not include the impact of unpredictable events, or black swans. Hence, the investors need to have a double dose of awareness – one for the pitfalls included in the mathematics of prediction that drive the models and one for black swans!

THE ILLUSTRATION TECHNIQUE

While detailed mathematical calculations can be used to bust each of the myths described in this book, this book is about myth busting in the classical sense. Hence, this book is not about mathematics, but about demonstrations that will show several commonly held beliefs in modern finance cannot possibly be true. The mathematics is, of course, available for anyone so inclined to check out the details.

The goal of the book is to illustrate each myth in as dramatic a fashion as possible with the use of actual data. It is hoped that by using this illustration approach, the true nature of what is happening in modern finance will become more visible and be understood by a larger audience. Although the illustrations will be few in number, and they have been selected for their ability to emphasize a key point, the illustrations do not depend on the data. Any other source of data (provided it is not a cannon ball and a feather pillow) will establish the same claim of falseness.

At times, the problem with a particular myth may be more easily seen if hypothetical data is used. In such cases hypothetical data will be selected to expose the problem as clearly as possible. However, hypothetical data will never be used to bust the myth. Hence, in this book in order for a modern finance myth to be busted, the demonstration must use realistic historical investment data. Hypothetical data may illustrate the point, but actual data will be used for the final dramatic demonstration.

The final demonstration data for this book all comes from the *Ibbotson SBBI 2008 Classic Yearbook – Market Results for Stocks, Bonds, Bills, and Inflation 1926 – 2007. (SBBI Yearbook)*. This excellent data source provides historical investment return information for a sample stock portfolio consisting of shares of stock invested primarily in larger companies, a separate sample portfolio for shares of stock invested primarily in smaller companies, as well as historical information for inflation and other investments.

This data source was selected because it is a large quantity of well-known and often-used data, which is very detailed and widely available. Copies of the *SBBI Yearbook* may be found in most major libraries. A summary of the *SBBI Yearbook* data, which will be critical in the myth busting demonstrations, is presented in the next chapter.

NECESSARY ARITHMETIC

There is one more little-known final myth which is part of the entire Galileo story. A student by the name of Skepticlius was one of the observers at Galileo's famous demonstration. Skepticlius was concerned that although the two objects dropped from the top of the Leaning Tower of Pisa appeared to be different in size, they might not be different in weight. Perhaps the larger object was hollowed out, so that in reality the two objects weighed the same. To guard against this possibility, Skepticlius brought his bathroom scale to the demonstration. After both objects went "thud" at the same time, Skepticlius was the first to retrieve them, and he then confirmed that the two objects did, in fact, have significantly different weights.

This myth highlights an interest that some readers may have in checking the details of any of the demonstrations presented in later chapters. For the most part, to be able to check any given demonstration one needs only to be able to perform three different mathematical tasks:

(a) Solve for the rate of return for a given period given only the beginning value and the ending value of the investment under consideration.

(b) Calculate the arithmetic mean for a set of rates of return determined for a given number of investment periods.

(c) Calculate the geometric mean rate of return for a particular investment.

These tasks are illustrated below so that interested readers will have the necessary tools to do their own checking. The illustration follows an investment of $1,300 as it goes up and down in value over a four-month period. The ending value of the investment is $1,450. A brief history of the investment is presented in Table 1.

Table 1

SAMPLE DATA FOR ILLUSTRATION PURPOSES

Month	Value at Start of Month	Value at End of Month
1	$1,300.00	$1,500.00
2	1,500.00	1,900.00
3	1,900.00	1,400.00
4	1,400.00	1,450.00

(a) The first task is to solve for the rate of return for each month. This task is completed in two steps. The first step is to determine the gain (loss) for the given month, and the second step is to divide that gain (loss) by the value of the investment at the start of the month. For example, the investment experienced a $200 gain in the first month as it grew from $1,300 to $1,500. Dividing $200 by the investment value of $1,300 at the start of the first month yields a 15.4% rate of return for the first month. As a second example, the investment experienced a $500 loss for the third month as it dropped in value from $1,900 to $1,400. Dividing this loss of $500 by the investment value of $1,900 at the start of the third month yields a

-26.3% rate of return for the third month. Table 2 below shows the rates of return for each of the four months.

Table 2

MONTHLY RATES OF RETURN

Month	Rate of Return
1	15.4%
2	26.7
3	-26.3
4	3.6

(b) The second task is to calculate the arithmetic mean of the above four numbers.

To get the arithmetic mean of a set of investment returns, one adds the returns, and divides by the number of elements in the sum. Sometimes the arithmetic mean is referred to as the average. In the illustration, the first step in determining the arithmetic mean is to add the four numbers shown above: $(15.4 + 26.7 - 26.3 + 3.6) = 19.4$. The second step is to then divide this sum by the number of months: $19.4/4 = 4.85\%$. Thus the arithmetic mean of the above four percentage returns is 4.85%.

(c) The third task is to calculate the geometric mean for the sample investment. The geometric mean is separate and distinct from the arithmetic mean. The two concepts are completely different. The geometric mean of an investment history is the single rate of return number, which if it had been earned for each of the periods, would have produced the same ending wealth as the actual investment.

Another way to look at the geometric mean is to use the four percentages that were determined in task (a) to note that if you had $1,300 at the start of a four month period, and earned

15.4% on the investment for the first month, 26.7% for the second month, lost 26.3% for the third month, and earned 3.6% for the last month, you would have $1,450 at the end of four months. The geometric mean then answers the question: If instead of having four different rates of return to achieve the ending value of $1,450, what single number used four times would you need to get to the same result?

One obvious candidate would be the 4.85% number that was just calculated as the arithmetic mean. But it turns out that this number is too large. If you start out with $1,300 and earn 4.85% for the first month you would have $1,363.05 at the end of the first month. At the end of the second month this amount grows to ($1,363.05) x (1.0485) = $1,429.16. By the end of the third month this amount grows to ($1,429.16) x (1.0485) = $1,498.47. And finally, by the end of the fourth month the original investment would have grown to ($1,498.47) x (1.0485) = $1,571.15. Since this ending result is larger than the actual ending result of $1,450, the 4.85% rate of return is too large.

One way to get the geometric mean would be through the use of trial and error. Just keep testing various possible candidates for a geometric mean until you find a rate that works. However, there is also a formula. It is a bit complicated but it always works. The geometric mean is obtained by taking the value of the investment at the end of the last period, dividing by the value of the investment at the beginning of the first period, and then raising this result to the power 1/n where n is the number of periods. This last result is then expressed as a percentage.

For the illustration above, the value of the investment at the end of the fourth month is $1,450, and the value of the investment at the start of the first month is $1,300. Dividing $1,450 by \$1,300 provides the following interim result: \$1,450/\$1,300 = 1.1154. Raising this number to the power ¼ yields: $(1.1154)^{1/4}$ = 1.0277. To get the percentage, the final step is to subtract the number one (1) and convert the remainder, in this case .0277, into a percentage or 2.77% monthly rate of return.

As noted before in this illustration, the geometric mean is less than the arithmetic mean. In fact this will always be the case when the investment does not grow at a uniform rate. The difference between geometric means and arithmetic means is an important factor in the myths that will be busted in the later chapters of this book.

While the geometric mean calculation process is somewhat cumbersome, the geometric mean provides a very valuable piece of information. This number is the rate of return, which if it had been earned each month, would have yielded the same ending wealth at the end of the four months that was achieved by the actual investment. The geometric mean tells the investor the average rate of return that he or she earned on the investment in terms of how much money was made throughout the entire four-month time frame. To illustrate this point, the following Table 3 is provided.

Table 3

GEOMETRIC MEAN CONFIRMING ILLUSTRATION

Month	Value at Start of Month	Value at End of Month	Rate of Return for Month
1	\$1,300.00	\$1,335.98	2.77%
2	1,335.98	1,372.95	2.77
3	1,372.95	1,410.95	2.77
4	1,410.95	1,450.00	2.77

The important point to keep in mind about the geometric mean is that it is a completely different calculation than the arithmetic mean. The word "mean" shows up in each verbal description, but they are very, very different calculations.

With that as background, the next chapter introduces the data that will be used as a key part of the myth-busting demonstrations included in *Six Myths in Modern Finance that Every Investor Needs to Know.*

Christopher Columbus Sets Sail for the New World

Chapter 2

THE IBBOTSON DATA

In fourteen hundred and ninety-two

Columbus sailed the ocean blue.

Seeking the East by heading west,

the "flat earth" myth, he did test.

Luckily for Chris and crew,

the "flat earth" myth was just not true.

THE ILLUSTRATION TECHNIQUE

The goal of *Six Myths in Modern Finance that Every Investor Needs to Know* is to highlight six key conclusions of modern finance that are not true. Once such a conclusion is identified, it will be labeled as a "myth," and then an illustration using actual data will be provided to demonstrate the problems with the conclusion.

The above technique of illustration does not have the dramatic flare that Galileo showed by dropping the objects from the Leaning Tower of Pisa, nor does it entail the risk encountered by Christopher Columbus when he sailed off into uncharted waters. However, the technique does have the potential to shine the light of truth on some very real problems and encourage further study in the field of modern finance. Given the problems experienced by this field in 2008, such additional scrutiny is certain to be welcomed by affected investors.

The claim that a modern finance conclusion is not true is based on detailed mathematical analysis as provided in the three published research papers mentioned in the Introduction. However, with very few exceptions, this book will limit the presentation to illustrations only. The goal of this book is to make the unreliability of the particular conclusion as visible to the average investor as possible. Since much of the mathematics that drive modern finance is highly sophisticated, converting these mathematical concepts into easily seen illustrations is a challenge.

The book has the additional goal of not only making the specific problem visible, but understandable as well. This task is harder. Liberal use of illustrations, such as the giant rotating bin of investment returns, will often be used. While the illustrations may seem simplistic or even humorous, the mathematical principles that created the concern and resulted in the labeling of a particular conclusion as a myth are very real. Unfortunately, many of the illustrations will involve numerical calculations. Working one's way through the details of a numerical chart is never easy, but those who take the time to do it may find that their understanding of a particular point will be enhanced.

Although the illustrations will be based on one or two sets of data, the particular point being made could be illustrated with a wide variety of data from any number of different sources. Since the point being made is purely mathematical in nature, virtually all data illustrations will tend to support the claim. The specific illustrations were certainly selected because they were deemed to illustrate the given point as clearly as possible.

However, in some cases it might be possible to find actual historical data, which due to unusual circumstances, may not support the given claim. This is not unlike the cannon ball and pillow example used to contradict Galileo's myth-busting demonstration. Just because such a non-confirming illustration may be found, it does not negate the mathematical point being illustrated. The Ibbotson data described below was selected because it is reasonable and appropriate for the task asked of it in this book.

THE ILLUSTRATION DATA

All of the data for illustrations used in this book will come from the *Ibbotson SBBI 2008 Classic Yearbook – Market Results for Stocks, Bonds, Bills, and Inflation 1926-2007. (SBBI Yearbook)* Ibbotson and Associates publishes the yearbook every spring with updated investment return information from the previous calendar year being added to the existing data set. The historical data is provided all the way back to January 1, 1926.

This chapter presents an overview of the Ibbotson data, showing clearly just how volatile the stock market has been. Investing in stocks has the potential to provide very handsome investment returns, but at the risk of large losses. The *SBBI Yearbook* includes historical investment return data for two different sample portfolios of stock. The first portfolio consists of stock investments primarily in larger companies. The second portfolio consists of stock investments primarily in smaller companies. The two different portfolios are included in the *SBBI Yearbook* to highlight the historical fact that returns for stock investments in smaller companies have tended to be larger, on average, than the returns for stock investments in larger companies.

You might think of either of these stock portfolios as being one of the diversified equity (stock) investment choices for your savings in your own 401(k) plan. The Ibbotson portfolios are effectively no different from one of these choices. The primary reason for using the Ibbotson data instead of data from a given fund, such as a Fidelity diversified equity fund or a Vanguard diversified equity fund, is that the Ibbotson data has a much longer detailed history. The longer history was selected only because of its increased volume, as having a large volume of data makes a graphical display much easier to see and understand. If you only have 10 data points, it is difficult to get much of a "feel" for the data from a graphical display.

The Ibbotson data shows historical investment performance month by month for each sample portfolio of stock investments. The data covers the period from January 1, 1926, to December 31, 2007 – 984 months in all. It is a lot of data! In addition to providing the monthly return data, the *SBBI Yearbook* accumulates these returns to create a stock return index for large company stock investments and a stock return index for small company stock investments. These indices are not dissimilar from any other market-based indices, such as the Dow Jones Industrial Average Index, the Standard & Poor's 500 Index, or the Russell 2000 Index.

In order to keep the data comparisons consistent and uniform, whenever an index is needed, the Ibbotson Indices will be used. Using the Ibbotson Indices instead of other common indices means that all the demonstrations will be based on a consistent data set. Readers will only need to gain an understanding of, and a feel for, two sets of data: the Ibbotson large company stock data and the Ibbotson small company stock data.

THE DISPLAY OF THE IBBOTSON DATA

The Ibbotson large company stock return data is displayed on pages 234 and 235 of the *SBBI Yearbook*. The data is displayed in 82 rows, one for each calendar year from 1926 through 2007. Each row contains 13 individual data elements. The first 12 data elements are the monthly returns listed for each month. Thus the first element listed is the rate of return for the month of January 1926. The second data element is the rate of return for the month of February 1926. The process continues across the row until the twelfth data element, which is the rate of return for December 1926.

The final element in each row is just the accumulated value of the previous 12 monthly returns. Thus, it shows the annual rate of return for the calendar year. The first 12 elements in each row are monthly returns, but the last element is an annual return.

The Ibbotson small company stock return data is displayed on pages 240 and 241 of the *SBBI Yearbook*. This data is displayed in exactly the same fashion as the large company data. Although it may seem like an insignificant point now, the display of the data in the *SBBI Yearbook* is actually a relevant point in the myth-busting demonstrations that occur later. Since the actual Ibbotson data is not included as part of this book, the above description of the data has been provided as necessary background.

IBBOTSON LARGE COMPANY STOCK RETURN DATA

Chart 1 shows the complete distribution of all 984 months of data and provides a graphical demonstration of the volatility inherent in stock investments. The bar on the left in Chart 1 shows that for 117 of the 984 months investors lost more than 4.2% just for the month. One can lose money investing in stocks. On the other hand, the bar on the right in Chart 1 shows that for 118 of the 984 months investors gained more than 5.8% just for the month. One can make money investing in stocks. The five bars in the middle provide information on the number of months that the rate of return was between -4.2% and 5.8% sorted into increments that are 2.0% wide. The rate range that had the largest number of months appears in the center of the chart. It is the rate range from -0.2% to 1.8%. The Ibbotson large company stock data show that 189 of the 984 months had returns that fell in this range.

Chart 1

DISTRIBUTION OF MONTHLY
LARGE COMPANYSTOCK RETURNS

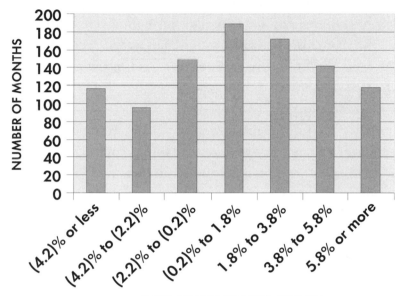

The above chart displays the distribution of Ibbotson large company stock returns in a graphical format. Some people are more comfortable with data displayed in a tabular format. For that reason, the table below provides the same information, but presents it in a different fashion.

117   The number of months between 1/1/26 and 12/31/07 when returns were less than -4.2%
 96   The number of months between 1/1/26 and 12/31/07 when returns were between -4.2% and -2.2%
150   The number of months between 1/1/26 and 12/31/07 when returns were between -2.2% and -0.2%
189   The number of months between 1/1/26 and 12/31/07 when returns were between -0.2% and 1.8%
172   The number of months between 1/1/26 and 12/31/07 when returns were between 1.8% and 3.8%
142   The number of months between 1/1/26 and 12/31/07 when returns were between 3.8% and 5.8%
118   The number of months between 1/1/26 and 12/31/07 when returns were 5.8% or more
984   The total number of months between 1/1/26 and 12/31/07

Some other interesting facts about the large company stock returns, which may be found by looking at the original source document but which do not show up in Chart 1, are as follows:

a)   The month that the large stock portfolio performed

the best was April 1933. For this month, the sample portfolio increased by 42.56% in just a single month. If you had had $1,000 invested in the portfolio at the start of that month, you would have had $1,426 by the end of the month.

b) On the flip side, the worst month was September 1931. For this month the sample large stock portfolio lost 29.73%. If you had had $1,000 invested in the portfolio at the start of that month, you would have only had $703 by the end of the month.

c) For 614 of the 984 months, the return for the month was greater than or equal to zero. This, of course, means that for 370 of the 984 months the return was negative. If one wants to invest in the stock market, one needs to be ready to endure months with negative returns.

d) Half of the months had a return greater than 1.31% for the month, and half of the monthly returns were less than this percentage.

The descriptions above reflect monthly stock returns instead of the more commonly used annual returns simply to increase the volume of data to be used in the illustrations. Using monthly data is conceptually no different from using annual data; however, having the larger volume of data just enhances the visual impact of charts such as Chart 1.

IBBOTSON SMALL COMPANY STOCK RETURN DATA

Some of the critical ideas presented in this book will be more easily demonstrated (have a visual impact more like Galileo's famous experiment) if the point is illustrated with data that is more variable (more spread out) than the data from the *SBBI Yearbook* for large company stock returns. For that reason, a specific point will often be illustrated twice, once using the large company stock data described above and once using the small company stock data from the same source.

The *SBBI Yearbook* includes 984 months of return data for a portfolio assumed to consist of stocks in smaller companies. The returns for these companies have tended to be much more variable over time than the returns for the larger companies. Chart 2 shows the complete distribution of the Ibbotson small company stock return data. Chart 2 is similar in general shape to Chart 1, but to accommodate the more variable data, the rate ranges for the five bars in the middle of the chart have been extended from 2.0% for large company stocks to 2.8% for small company stocks. As was the case with Chart 1, the largest number of months falls into the central rate range, in this case from -0.4% to 2.4%. For small stock returns, 207 of the total 984 months had a rate of return that fell in that rate range.

Chart 2

DISTRIBUTION OF MONTHLY
SMALL COMPANY STOCK RETURNS

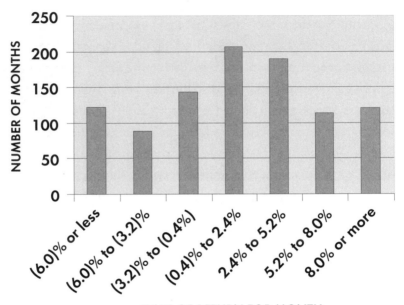

RATE OF RETURN FOR MONTH

The above chart displays the distribution of Ibbotson small company stock returns in a graphical format. Some people are more comfortable with data displayed in a tabular format. For that reason, the table below provides the same information, but presents it in a different fashion.

122 The number of months between 1/1/26 and 12/31/07 when returns were less than -6.0%
  88 The number of months between 1/1/26 and 12/31/07 when returns were between -6.0% and -3.2%
143 The number of months between 1/1/26 and 12/31/07 when returns were between -3.2% and -0.4%
207 The number of months between 1/1/26 and 12/31/07 when returns were between -0.4% and 2.4%
189 The number of months between 1/1/26 and 12/31/07 when returns were between 2.4% and 5.2%
114 The number of months between 1/1/26 and 12/31/07 when returns were between 5.2% and 8.0%
121 The number of months between 1/1/26 and 12/31/07 when returns were 8.0% or more
984 The total number of months between 1/1/26 and 12/31/07

Continuing the comparison with large company stock, the following additional points of interest are available from the original data, but do not show up in Chart 2:

a) The month that the small stock portfolio performed the best was August 1932. For this month, the sample portfolio increased by a whopping 73.46%, just for this single month. If you had had $1,000 invested in this portfolio at the start of the month, you would have had $1,735 by the end of the month.

b) On the flip side, the worst month was May 1940. For this month the sample small stock portfolio lost 36.74%. If you had had $1,000 invested in this portfolio at the start of the month, you would have only had $633 by the end of the month.

c) For 599 of the 984 months, the return for the month was greater than or equal to zero. This, of course, means that for 385 of the 984 months, the return for the month was negative.

d) Half of the months had returns greater than 1.4% for the month, and half of the months had returns less than this percentage. This number is greater than the 1.31% return for large company stocks noted above, but it comes with a much wider range of historical returns.

Comparing Chart 2 with Chart 1 shows that the small stock returns have a much wider distribution than the large stock returns. There are more months with very large returns, but also more months with very small (i.e., large negative!) returns. Generally, the variability of return rates has been considered to be reflective of the element of risk associated with the particular investment. Larger variability of returns reflects a larger element of risk. But with more risk comes more reward. Hence smaller company stocks (the comparatively more risky investment) have historically had larger average returns than larger company stocks (the comparatively less risky investment).

FLIPPING COINS

Using Charts 1 and 2 it is relatively easy to get a "feel" of how monthly returns have been distributed in the past. The very large positive returns and the very large negative returns have been fairly rare. It is more common to see returns near the center of each chart. This "feel" may serve as a guide for the anticipated distribution of future stock returns. It is actually charts like this that lead to modern finance in the first place. The shape of the data distribution as presented in Charts 1 and 2 looks somewhat like the distribution of possible results from a more classical probability distribution, such as flipping coins.

As a simple comparison, Chart 3 shows exactly that! Chart 3 shows the distribution of number of heads that were obtained by tossing 20 coins into the air and then counting the number of heads once they landed. The chart shows the distribution of the number of heads when the 20-coin-tossing experiment was repeated 984 times.

Chart 3

COIN FLIPPING EXPERIMENT WITH 20 COINS

DISTRIBUTION FOR THE NUMBER OF HEADS OUT OF 984 TRIALS OF THE EXPERIMENT

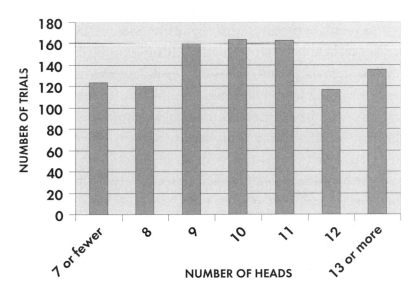

The experiment described by this chart involves throwing 20 coins into the air and then counting the number of heads once the coins land. The experiment was repeated 984 times, and the chart above shows the number of times (or trials) that the indicated number of heads was seen. Another way to describe the data is as follows:

124   The number of trials which had 7 or fewer heads
120   The number of trials which had exactly 8 heads
160   The number of trials which had exactly 9 heads
164   The number of trials which had exactly 10 heads
163   The number of trials which had exactly 11 heads
117   The number of trials which had exactly 12 heads
<u>136</u>   The number of trials which had 13 or more heads
984   The total number of times that 20 coins were tossed into the air

While the three charts, two showing historical investment returns and one showing the number of heads obtained from tossing coins into the air, are somewhat similar in shape, they are not identical, and the techniques of modern finance are more sophisticated than the techniques associated with simple coin flips. The biggest difference between the distributions of investment returns and the distribution of coin flips is that coin flipping may be fully and completely analyzed using the mathematical theory of probability.

Such is not the case with the distribution of investment returns. There is no mathematical theory of probability that permits the analysis of investment returns in the exactly the same fashion that coin flips may be analyzed. Charts 1 and 2 are developed from an actual investment history. Given that the mathematical theory of probability is not available as a tool to develop such charts, their analysis becomes more complex. Still, the basic theoretical conclusions used for coin flipping and investment returns are similar, and Chart 3 has been included to illustrate the relative closeness between the distribution of stock market returns and a more typical probability distribution. This topic is discussed in more detail in Chapter 5.

PERCENTAGE CHANCE QUESTIONS

Having a chart that shows a distribution of data makes it possible to answer questions about "percentage chance." For example, one might ask the question: If I threw 20 coins into the air, what is the percentage chance that 9 of them will be heads? From looking at Chart 3, one sees that 160 out of 984 trials produced this result. Assuming that the past coin flips present a reasonable basis for predicting the future, the chart then indicates that the percentage chance of getting 9 heads would be about 160/984 or 16.3%.

As a second example using the same chart, one might ask the question: If I threw 20 coins into the air, what is the percentage chance that the number of heads will be either 8 or 11? The chart shows that out of the 984 trials, 120 were trials with 8 heads, and 163 were trials with 11 heads. Thus 120 + 163 = 283 of the 984 trials had either 8 or 11 heads. Again making the assumption that this past demonstration provides a reasonable basis for predicting the future, this translates into a percentage chance of getting either 8 or 11 heads of about 283/984 or 28.8%.

With regard to investment returns, one might ask the question: What is the percentage chance that my investment in large company stocks will earn more than 5.8% for a given month? Using Chart 1, and assuming that the history displayed in Chart 1 provides reasonable estimates for the future, it is possible to answer this question. One notes that for 118 months out of the total of 984 months of data, the large company stock returns exceeded 5.8%. This information could then be expressed by saying that the percentage chance of earning 5.8% or more for a given month is about 118/984 or 12.0%.

As a second example, the percentage chance that an investment in large company stocks would return between 1.8% and 5.8% for any given month could be determined from the chart as follows. First note that 172 months out of the total of 984 months had returns between 1.8% and 3.8%, and that 142 months out of the total of 984 months had returns between 3.8% and 5.8%. Adding these two numbers together mean that 172 + 142 or 314 months out of the 984 total had a rate of return between 1.8% and 5.8%. Thus, based on this data the percentage chance of seeing a monthly rate of return between 1.8% and 5.8% on a large company stock investment becomes about 314/984 or 31.9%.

It is the answer to percentage chance questions about future investment returns and future account values that has been the big contribution of modern finance. The goal of providing such information is laudable. But it is critical that such information be as accurate as possible, so that investors will be making their decisions using the best available information.

ARITHMETIC MEANS AND
GEOMETRIC MEANS

The above sections have focused on the distribution of investment returns. It has been noted that there are relatively few very large monthly returns and relatively few very small (i.e., large negative) monthly returns. The observed investment returns tend to cluster around a central point.

While the distribution of returns is important, all investors are primarily interested in one goal – making money! Both sets of Ibbotson data clearly indicate the power of investing in the stock market and the power of compound interest. They show that a small investment left to earn compound interest for a long period of time can grow to be a sizeable amount of money. Expressing this growth as an average rate of return was discussed briefly at the end of Chapter 1. Since this point is so important, it will be discussed a second time below, but this time the discussion will be illustrated with the actual stock return data from the *SBBI Yearbook*.

Starting with a single $1.00 investment on January 1, 1926, the large company stock return data shows that this dollar would have grown to $1.00 by February 1, 1926. The return for the month of January turned out to be exactly 0%. However, in February 1926 things got worse. The return for that month was a loss of 3.85%, so the original dollar had shrunk to $0.96 by March 1, 1926. This process continues month after month. Actually by the end of 1926 the market had improved somewhat, so that by December 31, 1926, the original dollar was now worth $1.12.

All of these numbers seem on the small side. But give the markets time to work and great things can happen. This process of month after month compounding grows to the point that by January 1, 2007, the original dollar invested on January 1, 1926, was then worth $3,077.33. Factor in the growth for the 12 months of 2007, and by the end of 2007 the original January 1, 1926, dollar was worth $3,246.39. This 2007 growth occurred even though the months of February, June, July, November, and December all had negative returns.

As shown at the end of Chapter 1, there are two mathematically different ways to express this 82-year growth as an average annual investment return percentage. The first way, known as the arithmetic mean, uses the 82 calendar year returns as shown in the last column for each year in the display of the Ibbotson data (11.62% for 1926, 37.49% for 1927, etc., all the way up to 4.91% for 2005, 15.80% for 2006, and 5.49% for 2007) adds up all the numbers and divides by 82. This process yields an arithmetic mean return for the large company stock return data of 12.26%.

The second, more complicated, way to figure the average return is the geometric mean. The geometric mean uses the Ibbotson Index instead of each of the calendar year returns. The Ibbotson Index shows that $1.00 invested on January 1, 1926, would have grown to $3,246.39 by December 31, 2007. The geometric mean is determined by solving for the single rate of return, which would have reproduced this exact ending wealth on December 31, 2007, if this single rate had been compounded year after year. For the Ibbotson large company data, this single number is 10.36%.

Using the process described in Chapter 1 to calculate this number, one first divides the ending wealth, $3,246.39, by the beginning wealth, $1.00. In this case the answer is just the same number as the ending wealth or 3,246.39. The second step is then to raise this number to a power that is the number one (1) divided by the number of time periods for the wealth growth. In this case the number of time periods is 82 years, so the new exponent becomes 1/82. The actual calculation is then $3,246.39^{1/82} = 1.1036$. To get the geometric mean rate of return, you first subtract the number one (1), and convert the remainder, .1036, into a percentage. In this case the geometric mean rate of return is 10.36%.

In other words, if one had had one dollar invested on January 1, 1926, at this interest rate, it would have grown to $ 1.00 x (1.1036) = $ 1.1036 on January 1, 1927. This investment would have, in turn, grown to $ 1.1036 x (1.1036) = $ 1.2179 on January 1, 1928. Table 4 below shows this process continuing for several more years.

Table 4

ILLUSTRATION OF GEOMETRIC GROWTH

Year	Beginning of Year Value	Growth Rate for Year	End of Year Value
1926	$1.0000	1.1036	$ 1.1036
1927	1.1036	1.1036	1.2179
1928	1.2179	1.1036	1.3441
1929	1.3441	1.1036	1.4834
.	.	.	.
.	.	.	.
.	.	.	.
2005	2,415.2700	1.1036	2,665.4900
2006	2,665.4900	1.1036	2,941.6400
2007	2,941.6400	1.1036	3,246.3900

The above table shows the original dollar investment continuing to grow at the same rate of return until the investment reaches $ 3,246.39 on December 31, 2007. This is the same value that was obtained by investing in the Ibbotson large company stock portfolio for all 82 years.

Note that once again the geometric mean is less than the arithmetic mean. As pointed out before, this is always the case unless the rate of investment growth is completely uniform, and the importance of this difference is one of the key ideas to be continually illustrated in this book. Furthermore, the more variable the data, the greater the difference between geometric and arithmetic means. This point may be illustrated by looking at the corresponding calculations for the Ibbotson small company stock return data.

For the small company stock portfolio, the original $1.00 invested on January 1, 1926, would have grown to $15,091.10 by December 31, 2007. The arithmetic mean of the 82 calendar year returns is 17.08%. This number was obtained by adding together 82 different calendar year rates of return, and then dividing this sum by 82.

The geometric mean is obtained using only the beginning and ending values of the Ibbotson Index, the $1.00 at January 1, 1926, and the $15,091.10 at December 31, 2007. Dividing the ending value by the initial value, and then raising the resulting number to the 1/82 power produces the geometric mean of 12.45%. As noted before, the geometric mean of historical stock returns is always less than the arithmetic mean. Whereas the difference between the arithmetic mean and geometric mean was only about 2% for large company stock returns, it is more than 4% for small company stock returns. The more variable the data, the greater the difference between these two completely different mathematical ways of calculating average rates of return.

SUMMARY

This chapter has been devoted entirely to describing the raw investment return data. It shows that investing in stocks has the potential to provide great returns, but with a trade-off that there are bound to be some negative months and years along the way. The distribution of these various returns forms the basis for modern finance. Capturing this variability and providing data to investors based on this variability is the key contribution that modern finance has added to the investment process.

Now it is time to look at some of the key conclusions of modern finance that are simply not true, yet form the basis for some critical information provided to investors. Understanding these particular conclusions and learning why they are not true could impact how you use the techniques of modern finance to make your investment decisions.

Steve and Ziggy Analyze the Data

Chapter 3

MYTH 1: EVERY INVESTMENT HISTORY HAS A UNIQUE ANNUAL ARITHMETIC MEAN

Ziggy Zag and Steven Straight

are now engaged in hot debate.

Steven thinks one line will do,

while Ziggy favors twenty-two.

They'll toil away until quite late.

The final answer we all await.

MYTH 1: EVERY INVESTMENT HISTORY HAS A UNIQUE ANNUAL ARITHMETIC MEAN

The above myth was the first one to be selected for busting in this book for two reasons:

(1) It appears as if it cannot possibly be false; it seems as if an investment history MUST have a unique annual arithmetic mean.

(2) It appears in modern finance in several different and very important ways.

As an illustration of this second point, the next chapter deals with the myth that "the" arithmetic mean of annual investment return results is the best estimate for an expected annual rate of return in the future. If investment histories have more than one annual arithmetic mean, how will you know which one of these multiple arithmetic means is the true best estimate for the expected annual rate of return in the future? As a second example, and as will be shown in Chapter 6, "the" arithmetic mean of an investment history plays a significant role in the traditional process for estimating stock option prices. Again, if there are multiple arithmetic means, how will someone know which one is the correct one to use in stock option pricing?

Myth 1 is a key building block to many conclusions in academic finance. Busting this one myth will be a significant aid in busting several other myths. Given that each of these myths affects the everyday decisions of regular investors, the more investors understand about arithmetic means, and the limits of their usefulness, the better and wiser investors they will become.

In each of the above-cited examples the word "the" was put in quotation marks to highlight the fact that modern finance considers a given arithmetic mean or average to be unique. The myth-busting dramatic demonstration for this chapter will be to show that any given history does not have a single annual arithmetic mean, but that it has lots of them. Furthermore, the range of possible annual arithmetic means is sufficiently wide to cause an investor to seriously question the reliability of most of the commonly accepted arithmetic mean numbers.

BACKGROUND

On the surface it seems obvious that every investment history must have a unique arithmetic mean investment return. After all, in the previous chapter describing the Ibbotson large company stock return data, the calendar year arithmetic mean performance was stated to be 12.26%. How in the world could this not be the unique arithmetic mean of the Ibbotson large company data? One merely adds up 82 individual numbers, divides the total by 82, and gets the one and only answer. In this case the one and only answer has to be 12.26%. Badda bing, badda boom!

But as has been shown in the past, sometimes things that seem obvious at first turn out to be a lot more complex. As will be shown below, the key problem with the normal procedure for calculating an annual arithmetic mean is that an awful lot of useful investment return data is not used at all as part of the process. Before describing the data that is discarded, and the impact it has on the Ibbotson calculation, it is helpful to clearly see the problem by looking at simple hypothetical example.

Consider the case of Dave and Deana from Denver who will appear from time to time in this book. Whenever an investment is needed to illustrate a key point, Dave and Deana will have made exactly this investment. Furthermore, they are very serious about their investing and have maintained meticulous records. To illustrate the problem of discarded data and the impact it has on arithmetic means (average returns), consider the investment of $1,000 that Dave and Deana made on February 17, 2003. By August 17, 2008, this investment had grown to $1,378.

The geometric mean return for this investment, which describes the actual rate of growth of the investment in terms of how much money Dave and Deana actually made, is obtained by taking the ending value, $1,378, dividing by the beginning value, $1,000, and raising the result to a power equal to the number one (1) divided by the length of time the money was invested, in this case 5.5 years. The actual calculation becomes $(1,378/1,000)^{1/(5.5)}$ or 6.0% per year. Thus, with this investment Dave and Deana wound up with the exact ending wealth as if they had been invested in a certificate of deposit that paid interest at a constant rate of 6.0% per year for the 5.5 year period. However, out of curiosity, on one Friday night Dave and Deana decide to calculate the arithmetic mean return for this investment.

The first thing to notice is that Dave and Deana have a very difficult challenge. If they have only the beginning investment value, in this case the $1,000, and only the ending value, in this case $1,378, they cannot calculate any arithmetic mean, let alone a unique one. Without intermediate observations of how the investment changed over the five and a half years, it is absolutely impossible to calculate an arithmetic mean.

But even if Dave and Deana have lots of intermediate information, the calculation of the arithmetic mean is anything but a slam dunk. Continuing the illustration, Dave and Deana each reach for the entire file concerning the history of the investment. This information is presented in Chart 4. Armed with this added information, they each head to their own personal computer to create a spreadsheet. The goal: Find the arithmetic mean of this investment.

Chart 4
DAVE AND DEANA'S INVESTMENT

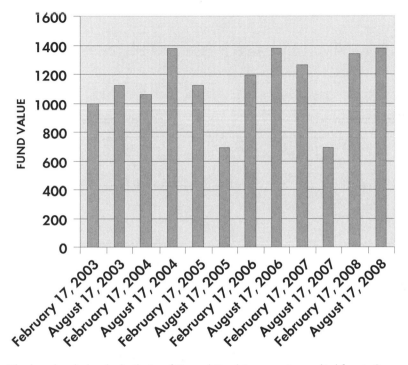

The above chart displays the distribution of Dave and Deana's Investment in a graphical format. Some people may prefer an actual table of results. For that reason the following actual history is also provided.

Date	Fund Value	Date	Fund Value	Date	Fund Value
2/17/03	$1,000.00	2/17/05	$1,123.60	2/17/07	$1,262.48
8/17/03	1,122.73	8/17/05	689.00	8/17/07	689.00
2/17/04	1,060.00	2/17/06	1,191.02	2/17/08	1,338.23
8/17/04	1,378.00	8/17/06	1,378.00	8/17/08	1,378.00

Dave decides that in order to calculate an annual arithmetic mean, he needs to know the value of the investment at annual intervals. For his annual intervals Dave selects the period from February 17 of one year to February 17 of the next. He looks up the historical information for February 17, 2004,

2005, 2006, 2007, and 2008. His spreadsheet is presented in Table 5 as follows:

Table 5

DAVE'S CALCULATION OF ARITHMETIC MEAN

Date	Value at Date	Value 1 Year Later	Rate of Return
2/17/03	$1,000.00	$1,060.00	6.0%
2/17/04	1,060.00	1,123.60	6.0
2/17/05	1,123.60	1,191.02	6.0
2/17/06	1,191.02	1,262.48	6.0
2/17/07	1,262.48	1,338.23	6.0
2/17/08	1,338.23	N/A	N/A
8/17/08	1,378.00		
Arithmetic Mean Rate of Return (Average of Last Column):			6.0%

Dave notices that for the short 6-month period from February 17, 2008, to August 17, 2008, the investment grew from $1,338.23 to $1,378.00. This change in value is about 3.0% which is consistent with Dave's arithmetic mean from the above spreadsheet, given that short period was exactly one half of a year. He concludes that the investment had an arithmetic mean of 6.0% and he is happy.

Deana also figured out that in order to calculate an annual arithmetic mean she needed to use data at annual intervals. However, she selected years running from August 17 of one year to August 17 of the next. She looked up historical information for August 17, 2003, 2004, 2005, 2006, and 2007. Deana's spreadsheet is shown in Table 6 as follows:

Table 6

DEANA'S CALCULATION OF
ARITHMETIC MEAN

Date	Value at Date	Value 1 Year Later	Rate of Return
2/17/03	$1,000.00	N/A	N/A
8/17/03	1,122.73	$1,378.00	22.7%
8/17/04	1,378.00	689.00	-50.0
8/17/05	689.00	1,378.00	100.0
8/17/06	1,378.00	689.00	-50.0
8/17/07	689.00	1,378.00	100.0
8/17/08	1,378.00		
Arithmetic Mean Rate of Return (Average of Last Column):			24.5%

Deana noticed that for the short six-month period from February 17, 2003, to August 17, 2003, the investment grew from $1,000.00 to $1,122.73. This change in value is about 12.27% which is consistent with Deana's arithmetic mean from the above spread sheet, given that the short period was exactly one half of a year. She concluded that the investment had an arithmetic mean of 24.5% and she was happy.

Both of the above spreadsheets are 100% correct. Because Dave's goal was to calculate an annual arithmetic mean, he selected interim dates that were one year apart. He selected annual periods running from one February 17 to the next February 17, and his worksheet only reflects the value of the investment on the dates he selected. His calculation ignored all the other information available, including the wide swings which showed up each August.

The same basic dynamic occurs with Deana's calculation. She also selected interim dates that were one year apart, running from each August 17 to the next August 17. The selection of these particular dates caused her to ignore all the other available information. The resulting difference in the answers is huge: 6.0% vs. 24.5%. Taking the annual arithmetic mean of historical data by only looking at a snapshot of the data once every 12 months means that a lot of available information will be missed in any given calculation. This process can lead to a very wide range of possible answers as in the Dave and Deana example.

This illustration highlights the technique that will be used to bust Myth 1 using the Ibbotson data. The dramatic myth busting illustration to show that Myth 1 is, in fact, false is to show that the Ibbotson investment history has lots of arithmetic means, and that these arithmetic means have a fairly wide range in values.

THE *SBBI YEARBOOK* ARITHMETIC MEAN

The *SBBI Yearbook* shows an 82-year arithmetic mean of 12.26%, and only this number, when describing the Ibbotson large company stock return data. But as in the Dave and Deana illustration, this number only reflected a very limited selection of all the information available. In particular it only reflects the values of the Ibbotson Index as of each December 31. All other Ibbotson Index values are completely ignored. Any wide swings in the growth of the Ibbotson Index that occur during a calendar year would have no affect on the calculated 12.26% arithmetic mean.

While this seems pretty straight forward and seems to indicate that the arithmetic mean must be 12.26%, the key point is that this result did not come from the historical performance itself, but was based on the decision made by Ibbotson and Associates to select Index values at the beginning and end of each calendar year for measuring the rate of return for the year.

This process could have been just as easily applied to periods other than calendar years. While it might be thought that selecting other fiscal periods would produce the same or similar answers, this is not the case. Each different fiscal period will yield a different arithmetic mean.

GROUPING THE DATA BY FISCAL YEAR

The monthly data as presented in the *SBBI Yearbook* is grouped and summarized in calendar year increments. But as noted above, the decision to group the data in this fashion was made by someone at Ibbotson and Associates, not the market. In particular, since the Ibbotson data is monthly in nature, someone could have made the decision to group the data by fiscal years ending each June 30, instead of by calendar year. The annual returns would have been measured taking changes in the Ibbotson Index from a fiscal year that begins on July 1 of a given calendar year and ends on June 30 of the following calendar year. The resulting rates of return are still annual returns, but they are annual returns for the fiscal years ending June 30 instead of for calendar years.

Providing reasonable adjustment, such as a one-half weighting, for the two short fiscal years (January 1, 1926 – June 30, 1926, and July 1, 2007 – December 31, 2007), this process produces a second arithmetic mean for the Ibbotson data – one based on fiscal years ending on June 30. This arithmetic mean is 13.30%, a number that is more than 1% larger than the 12.26% value stated in the yearbook. While many may not consider this to be a "dramatic" change, it still is a change. Hence, the stated 12.26% number is not unique. For completeness, Table 7 below shows the full range of fiscal year arithmetic means.

Table 7

ARITHMETIC MEANS FOR LARGE COMPANY STOCK RETURNS

Fiscal Year Ending	Arithmetic Mean Percentage
January	12.32%
February	12.51
March	12.98
April	12.58
May	13.16
June	13.30
July	12.50
August	12.23
September	12.35
October	12.00
November	12.14
December	12.26

Note that each of these fiscal year calculations uses the same data as the calendar year results presented in the previous chapter. Each of the above arithmetic means is determined for an investment that has an initial value of $1.00 on January 1, 1926 and ends with a value of $3,246.39 on December 31, 2007. The only change has been to rearrange the display of the data so that it is displayed by fiscal year and to provide for a reasonable weighting of the two short fiscal years, one in 1926 and one in 2007.

The arithmetic means (or average returns) range from a low of 12.00% for the fiscal years ending in October to a high of 13.30% for the fiscal years ending in June. Clearly, how Ibbotson and Associates chooses to arrange the data has an impact on the annual "arithmetic mean" disclosed in their yearbook. Thus, historical data does not have a unique annual arithmetic mean return; it has at least 12 of them!

SMALL COMPANY STOCK ILLUSTRATION

The same illustration described above may also be completed for the Ibbotson portfolio of small company stocks. Since this data is more variable than the large company stock data, this same variability is likely to carry over to the arithmetic means calculated for various fiscal years. It is common in modern finance to describe "the" arithmetic mean of such data using only calendar year increments. This produces "the" arithmetic mean of 17.08% cited in the *SBBI Yearbook*. Table 8 below provides a much more complete picture.

Table 8

ARITHMETIC MEANS OF SMALL COMPANY STOCK RETURNS

Fiscal Year End	Mean Return Percentage
January	17.49%
February	18.49
March	19.35
April	18.31
May	18.95
June	19.02
July	16.99
August	15.94
September	16.05
October	15.84
November	16.47
December	17.08

As shown above, arithmetic means of the small company stock data range from a low of 15.84% for fiscal years ending in October to a high of 19.35% for fiscal years ending in March. This result is somewhat wider than the 12.0% to 13.3% range shown for the large company stock returns and could actually begin to impact investor behavior.

Had investors been told that the arithmetic mean of small company stock returns was 15.84% instead of 17.08%, they might have been less inclined to invest in small company stocks. On the other hand, if the investors had been told that the historical arithmetic mean returns for small company stocks had averaged 19.35% instead of 17.08%, they might have been more inclined to invest in small company stocks.

Yet there is no particular reason for picking any one of the above arithmetic means over any of the others. The market itself does not rise up on each December 31, wave a big red flag, and shout: "Now is the 'right' time to measure stock market rates of return." The common practice of measuring these rates on a calendar year basis is just that – a common practice. As shown above, this common practice may be providing investors with information that might not be as full and compete as it could be.

Keep in mind one final time that every single one of the above numbers is based on the same set of data. In every case the original dollar invested on January 1, 1926, is still worth $15,091.10 on December 31, 2007. The only difference between any of the numbers is the selection of the fiscal year used to group the data. In other words, how the data is displayed in the *SBBI Yearbook*.

ANNUAL ARITHMETIC MEANS BASED ON SHORTER TIME FRAMES

While the above sections clearly bust the claim of Myth 1, that the annual arithmetic mean is a unique number, the goal of this book is to provide a fuller and more complete picture of the impact that the mathematics of modern finance may have on actual investors. For that reason, this chapter will provide the following additional information about an arithmetic mean of an investment history.

The reason that the above different fiscal year calculations provided different arithmetic means is that for each of the calculations, a significant portion of the data is tossed away. For example, in the original 12.26% Ibbotson large company stock return arithmetic mean calculation, only 82 different Ibbotson index values were used (one for each calendar year end), when 984 were available. Ninety-two percent of the available data was ignored!

In order to capture this extra data, it is possible to calculate an annual arithmetic mean rate of return in a very different way. Instead of ignoring 92% of the data, this process will use all 984 of the Ibbotson index values. Using this process, one first takes the arithmetic mean or average of all the monthly returns provided in the *SBBI Yearbook*. This monthly average is then converted into (or expressed as) an annual equivalent rate of return. This process uses all of the listed Ibbotson index figures, not just a small fraction of them.

For the large company stock returns, the arithmetic mean of the monthly data is 0.9754%. This result is simply obtained by adding up all 984 monthly returns and dividing that total by 984. If an investment earns this 0.9754% rate of return each month for 12 months, the rate of return for the year will be 12.35%. This process is referred to as converting the monthly rate of 0.9754% into an annual equivalent rate of 12.35%. Using this process, one could say that the annual arithmetic mean for large company stocks was 12.35%. It is just that this annual arithmetic mean was based on monthly observations. For the small company stock returns the arithmetic mean of the monthly data is 1.3207%, which converts to an annual equivalent rate of return of 17.05%. Again, one could then say that the annual arithmetic mean for small company stocks was 17.05% but that this annual arithmetic mean was based on monthly observations.

Some people may be uncomfortable referring to an "annual" arithmetic mean, when the data that was used to calculate it was monthly in nature. To help relieve some concern in this area, think about the answer to the question: How fast are you driving your car? If someone asks you this question while you are actually driving, your normal response is to look at your speedometer and report the speed as something like 45 miles per hour.

By reporting the speed as "45 miles per hour" you are not stating that you actually drove 45 miles, or that you actually spent one hour doing it. You were describing the speed at which you were driving at the time the question was asked using commonly understood terminology. In the same way, describing the monthly returns as 12.35% per year uses annual terminology to describe the arithmetic mean of monthly returns.

Because each of these new annual equivalent rates of return (one for large company stock returns and one for small company stock returns) reflect observations from 984 data points (one for each month) instead of 82 data points (one for each year), there may be some comfort to the idea that this number is somehow more accurate because of the increased number of observations. The reason Dave's calculation turned out to only be 6.0% in the Dave and Deana illustration is because the dates that Dave selected caused Dave to miss all the high and low values for the investment. By using the revised process the chance that the highs and lows might be missed is significantly reduced, since the revised process uses many more data points.

But anyone who watches a business news program on television is now keenly aware that data is available much more frequently than monthly. Often there is a little window on the television screen which shows the current Dow Jones Industrial Average (DJIA) value. This number changes every few seconds. If one calculated an annual Dow Jones Industrial Average arithmetic mean by just using month-end data, he or she would be throwing away millions of pieces of information as to how the DJIA changed over the course of a year.

This raises a question: Is it possible to calculate an arithmetic mean which captures as much of this data as possible? The surprising answer is yes! It is possible to calculate an arithmetic mean which reflects absolutely every single change in an index such as the Ibbotson Index or the DJIA, or even every single transaction involving an individual share of stock. This calculation process is described below.

"ARITHMETIC MEANS" FROM CONTINUOUS GROWTH

Given that using monthly data to calculate an annual rate of return still means that millions of pieces of information will be lost, the idea of using even smaller time increments, such as a week, a day, or even an hour, might be considered as a possible time period for figuring an arithmetic mean that could then be converted into an annual equivalent rate of return. The concept of calculating arithmetic means by using more data points and then converting the results to annual equivalents has a good feel about it. Somehow using more and more data gives one the feeling that the result may be more accurate than if just a limited number of observations of the wealth growth are used.

It turns out that figuring out the arithmetic mean of returns taken over very small time frames is not as difficult as one might think. The first step is to consider how the value of a stock is determined and how this value changes over time. These values and changes are determined by actual investors, just like you.

For example, assume that Allen in Altoona decides to enter into a transaction to buy a particular stock at $20 per share at exactly 1:00:00 p.m. on October 1, 2008. This action by Allen then sets the value of the stock at $20, until 8 seconds later when Bob in Boston agrees to a transaction at $20.50 per share. Thus, $20.50 becomes the new value. At exactly 1:00:24 Cheryl in Chicago makes the next transaction for shares at a price of $20.25. This process continues on and on and on. The stock market in action is truly a marvel to behold.

Chart 5 shows one minute's worth of these transactions. As noted above, the first two transactions were 8 seconds apart and the next two were 16 seconds apart. The timing between other transactions ranges from 4 seconds to 20 seconds. Chart 5 also illustrates a significant problem if one tried to calculate an arithmetic mean rate of return based on changes in share value calculated over one second time intervals. What would be the share value for times like 1:00:01, 1:00:02, and 1:00:03 when no transactions occurred?

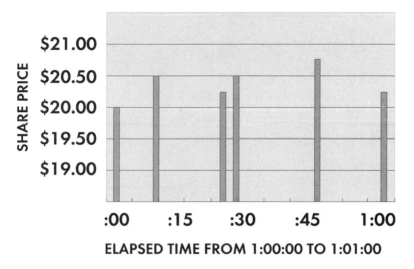

Chart 5
STOCK PURCHASE PRICE HISTORY

This chart displays the share prices from all the transactions for a given share that occurred between 1:00:00 on October 1, 2008, and 1:01:00 on October 8, 2008. There were 6 transactions in all ranging in price from $20.00 per share to $20.75 per share.

The answer to this is really quite simple. Just draw a nice smooth line that connects every single one of the actual transactions! Chart 6 shows how this can be done. Note that the smooth line just fills in the gaps between two actual transactions, and it fills in the gaps using reasonable values for the share price. Using this new line, a person can estimate the value for the stock for any point in time, even times when no transaction occurred. This process just provides for a reasonable transition from one transaction to the next. While this book is not about mathematics, for the curious, Appendix 1 contains a mathematical proof that this smooth line can always be drawn. This line is what is known in mathematics as a "continuous and differentiable" curve.

Chart 6

STOCK PURCHASE PRICE HISTORY

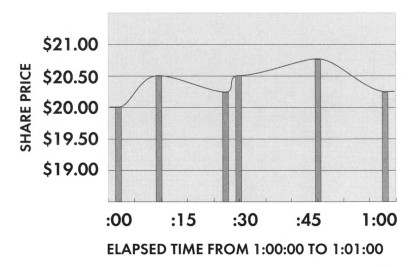

This chart displays the share prices from all the transactions for a given share that occurred between 1:00:00 on October 1, 2008, and 1:01:00 on October 8, 2008. There were 6 transactions in all ranging in price from $20.00 per share to $20.75 per share.

The chart contains the same basic information as found in Chart 5. However, Chart 6 has been modified to include a continuous and differentiable curve that connects all the data points reflecting actual transactions. This curve provides approximate share prices for times when no actual transactions occurred.

While it is not common in modern finance to consider such curves when thinking about or calculating average returns, the concept is really quite logical. The curve passes through the data point for every single transaction of the stock! Not one single transaction is missed. The smooth curve is used only to fill in the gaps between any two successive transactions. And the gaps are always filled with reasonable stock values, which are in between the two actual transactions at each end of the gap.

Assuming that stock price changes may be described by a continuous and differentiable curve, it is now possible to calculate an annual arithmetic mean that reflects absolutely every transaction for the stock. This new annual arithmetic mean is just the annual equivalent of an arithmetic mean of historical results taken over very, very small time frames. Using all of the data, instead of just a minor portion of it, seems to provide additional assurance that one is getting the "right" answer.

The current method of calculating an annual arithmetic mean as shown in the *SBBI Yearbook* uses just 82 data items from the historical record. That's all, just 82 separate pieces of data. If the process is expanded to monthly, then 984 pieces of information contribute to the calculation process. If the annual arithmetic mean is determined by taking daily snapshots of what was happening to the Ibbotson Index, then the calculation would have over 20,000 data elements. But even with daily numbers, the calculations would still miss all the market changes that occur within a single day.

If the calculations were carried out by taking the arithmetic mean of the rates of return over 1/10 of one second time intervals, the total volume of information would be over 5 billion individual observations of market behavior! It just seems natural that this result would have to be a far more accurate measure of the annual arithmetic mean than the relatively crude 82 element calculation process that is currently used.

There is an amazing answer that results from calculating the arithmetic mean or average of these 5 billion rates of return calculated over 1/10 of one second time intervals and then expressing this arithmetic mean as an annual rate of return. This amazing answer is that this process yields the geometric mean!

In other words, if the arithmetic mean calculation process used absolutely every single transaction, and then only filled in the gaps between transactions with a reasonable curve with values between the two actual transaction values, the annual equivalent of the resulting arithmetic mean is the geometric mean.

Using only a limited number of data snapshots from the historical record produces an array of arithmetic means, all of which are larger than the geometric mean. Again for the curious, a mathematical proof of this point is included as Appendix 1.

INVESTOR IMPACT

The above information now expands the possible range for arithmetic means for Ibbotson large company stock returns from the geometric mean of 10.36%, which is based on billions of data point observations, to 13.30%, which is based on 82 observations taken as of each June 30. The value of $10,000 invested for 20 years at these two rates ranges from $71,818 to $121,506.

With respect to Ibbotson small company stock returns, the complete range of possible arithmetic means runs from the geometric mean of 12.45%, which is based on billions of data point observations, to 19.35%, which is based on 82 observations taken as of each March 30. The value of a $10,000 invested for 20 years at these two rates ranges from $104,518 to $343,913. In short, the dramatic differences are beginning to show up.

CONCLUSION

The important point to be taken from Myth 1 is that any particular history of investment fund performance has lots of arithmetic means, and as shown above, these means can differ significantly. Any time in modern finance, if one sees a reference to "the" arithmetic mean of a data set, watch out! The asserted result is heavily dependent on which of the various arithmetic means was used. In particular, while the calendar year arithmetic mean of the 82-year historical large company Ibbotson data is, in fact, 12.26%, using an alternative, yet still equally valid approach to calculating an arithmetic mean, this result could have varied anywhere from a low of 10.36% to a high of 13.3%. And it is particularly significant that the arithmetic mean based on the most data is the 10.36% number.

Revisiting the Dave and Deana illustration one more time, one can note that Dave's calculated arithmetic mean matched the geometric mean for the investment. In short, in terms of real money, Dave and Deana's investment actually had a 6.0% rate of return. It is interesting to ponder the question: Are Dave and Deana out in a tavern boasting about their fantastic 24.5% arithmetic mean as calculated by Deana, or are they quietly accepting the fact that the investment only had a 6% return. If someone tells an investor to consider investing in a stock because it had a 25% arithmetic mean return, the investor is probably well advised to ask more questions!

Fred Franklin, C.P.A. Finds Fame

Chapter 4

MYTH 2: THE ANNUAL ARITHMETIC MEAN OF HISTORICAL RETURNS IS THE BEST ESTIMATE FOR THE EXPECTED RATE OF RETURN FOR THE COMING YEAR

Little-known Fred is a great C.P.A.;

who once every year has a very big day.

He gives a big spin and then reaches in

to see if savers might lose or might win.

MYTH 2: THE ANNUAL ARITHMETIC MEAN OF HISTORICAL RETURNS IS THE BEST ESTIMATE FOR THE EXPECTED RATE OF RETURN FOR THE COMING YEAR

Given the demonstration presented in Myth 1, and the use of the word "the" at the start of Myth 2, the above advice cannot possibly be true. Yet, Myth 2 is commonly seen in finance textbooks that are used at major universities. The advice provided by Myth 2 has become so sufficiently well-known that it seems appropriate to allow this myth to have its own separate chapter.

The 12 fiscal year-end arithmetic means used in the large company illustration in the last chapter ranged from 12.0% to 13.3%. Yet there is no particular reason that any number in that range is any more of a "best estimate" than any other number in the range. Each of the calculations used only 82 specific observations of actual market value; the different dates used in taking the annual snapshots of the market accounting for the different annual arithmetic means. Furthermore, when the concept of annual arithmetic mean is expanded to reflect billions of snapshots that would provide for a more accurate measure, the annual arithmetic mean gets lowered to the geometric mean of 10.36%.

The 12 fiscal year-end arithmetic means used in the small company illustration had an even broader range, 15.84% to 19.35%. Yet once again, there is no reason to conclude that any particular number in that range is more of a "best estimate" than any other number in the range. Each calculation only reflects 82 specific values with the range of arithmetic means just being a byproduct of the different dates being selected for measuring annual returns. Using the expanded arithmetic mean concept to reflect billions of snapshots, the annual arithmetic mean gets lowered to the geometric mean of 12.45%.

Furthermore, the Ibbotson data show that for the past 82 years, the average rate of growth (geometric mean) for the sample portfolio of large company stocks has been 10.36%, and the average rate of growth (geometric mean) for the sample portfolio of small company stocks has been 12.45%. Keep in mind that these two numbers are relevant when thinking about the really important question: How much money did I make on my investment?

In spite of this, modern finance asks investors to believe that somehow, magically, next year's return is expected to be significantly better than these very long-term growth rates. And to make matters even stranger, this better number (somewhere between 12.0% and 13.3% for large company stocks, and between 15.84% and 19.35% for small company stocks) is based solely on the data that produces either the 10.36% or 12.45% long-term average return in the first place!

Although Myth 2 has been busted right out of the gate, the above points raise the very important question: How did modern finance reach the conclusion presented in Myth 2 in the first place? To answer this question and provide more detail for later myth-busting illustrations, it is necessary to turn one more time to the giant rotating bin of stock market returns.

ROTATING BINS WITH ONLY
TWO POSSIBLE RETURNS

To illustrate the source of Myth 2, it is easiest to start with a rotating bin that has only two balls in it. This bin is modeling a market situation where the particular investment is equally likely to provide a return at either of the two numbers written on the balls. In this first illustration these numbers will be 5% and 25%. Hence, for a given year the investment is assumed to return one of these two rates, and that only these two results are possible.

If a person makes a $100 investment using this model, at the end of one year the person will have either $105, if the 5% ball gets drawn, or $125, if the 25% ball gets drawn. Since each of these choices is equally likely, it is common to say that the average ending wealth after one year will be ($105 + $125)/2 or $115. Note that it is the arithmetic mean of 5% and 25%, which is 15%, that is the rate of return that will yield this average ending wealth.

Expanding the concept to a two-year investment horizon just increases the number of equally likely possibilities for ending wealth. Table 9 below shows the full range of possible two-year outcomes for a $100 investment.

Table 9

$100 INVESTMENT USING ONLY TWO RETURNS

Year 1 Return	Year 2 Return	Wealth at Year 1	Ending Wealth
5.0%	5.0%	$105.00	$110.25
5.0	25.0	105.00	131.25
25.0	5.0	125.00	131.25
25.0	25.0	125.00	156.25
Average Ending Wealth			$132.25

Again, the arithmetic mean of 5% and 25%, which is 15%, is the rate that reproduces the average ending wealth of the four equally likely possible choices. $100 x (1.15) x (1.15) = $132.25.

If the illustration were expanded to reflect a 3-year investment horizon, the number of equally likely possibilities for ending wealth grows to eight. Table 10 below shows the full range of equally likely possible three-year outcomes for the $100 investment.

Table 10

$100 INVESTMENT USING ONLY TWO RETURNS

Year 1 Return	Year 2 Return	Year 3 Return	Wealth at Year 1	Wealth at Year 2	Ending Wealth
5.0%	5.0%	5.0%	$105.00	$110.25	$115.76
5.0	5.0	25.0	105.00	110.25	137.81
5.0	25.0	5.0	105.00	131.25	137.81
25.0	5.0	5.0	125.00	131.25	137.81
5.0	25.0	25.0	105.00	131.25	164.06
25.0	5.0	25.0	125.00	131.25	164.06
25.0	25.0	5.0	125.00	156.25	164.06
25.0	25.0	25.0	125.00	156.25	195.31
Average Ending Wealth					$152.09

Once again, it is the arithmetic mean of 5% and 25% that is the unique rate of return that will reproduce the average ending wealth. In this case $100 x (1.15) x (1.15) x (1.15) = $152.09. It is this point, that the arithmetic mean is the answer that reproduces the average ending wealth, which drives Myth 2.

Adding more balls to the bin or expanding the investment horizon to more years is conceptually no different. With more balls in the rotating bin or a longer investment horizon, the number of different possible outcomes just becomes larger. But in all cases the arithmetic mean of the numbers on the balls will be the rate that will reproduce the average ending wealth. If investing truly consisted of drawing balls out of a rotating bin, this result makes complete sense. But it is important to keep in mind that we are talking about real investments, not just theoretical models.

Later in this chapter we consider the problems with this rotating bin model when confronted with actual historical investment return data. However, before leaving the simple two-choice illustration, it is helpful to look at a couple more specific two-choice cases. In each case the arithmetic mean is still 15%, just as above, but the two rates that have this arithmetic mean will no longer be 5% and 25%, but will be numbers that are farther apart. The first case uses rates of -41.8% and 71.8%. The results are presented in Table 11 below.

Table 11
$100 INVESTMENT USING ONLY
TWO RETURNS

Year 1 Return	Year 2 Return	Wealth at Year 1	Ending Wealth
-41.8%	-41.8%	$58.20	$33.87
-41.8	71.8	58.20	100.00
71.8	-41.8	171.80	100.00
71.8	71.8	171.80	295.13
Average Ending Wealth			$132.25

The average ending wealth is the same as in the first two-choice illustration, and the arithmetic mean of the two possible choices, 15%, is still the rate of return which reproduces this ending wealth. However, now any of the hoped for gain is concentrated in a single large return which would occur when the larger of the two assumed investment returns occurs two years in a row. The other three possibilities all result in ending wealth where the investor either loses money on the investment or just breaks even, notwithstanding the 15% rate of return for the average ending wealth.

This illustration highlights a very key point about interest rates. Note that it takes a 71.8% increase to bring a $100 investment up to $171.80, but only a 41.8% decrease to bring it back to $100. The same process works in reverse as well. While it only takes a 41.8% decrease to lower a $100 investment to $58.20, it takes a 71.8% increase to bring the investment back to its original $100 level.

This dynamic always happens. A 10% decrease requires an 11% increase to get back to the original starting point. A 25% increase requires a 20% decrease to get back to the original starting point. A 33% decrease requires a 50% increase to get back to the original starting point. In all cases, and no matter whether the increase comes first or the decrease comes first, it takes a larger increase to off set the impact of a specific decrease.

The next illustration takes the issue of two interest rates that are far apart to its extreme by using the rates of -100% and 130%, two rates which still have an arithmetic mean of 15%. The results are presented in Table 12 below.

Table 12

$100 INVESTMENT USING ONLY
TWO RETURNS

Year 1 Return	Year 2 Return	Wealth at Year 1	Ending Wealth
-100.0%	-100.0%	$0.00	$0.00
-100.0	130.0	0.00	0.00
130.0	-100.0	230.00	0.00
130.0	130.0	230.00	529.00
Average Ending Wealth			$132.25

As before, the average ending wealth is still $132.25, and it is the arithmetic mean of the two interest rates (-100% + 130%)/2 = 15% that reproduces the average ending wealth.

In this case all possibilities are zero, except the extreme case where the two great years come back to back. Now it is time to see how these simple theoretical illustrations are affected when one is dealing with actual historical data.

USING ACTUAL HISTORICAL TWO-YEAR DATA

The above illustrations were hypothetical in nature. They assumed that someone "knew" what the two possible interest rates would be. In the real world, no one "knows" what these rates are, so it has been common to turn to actual historical results to get the numbers that are written on the balls in the giant rotating bin. Before proceeding to more complex cases with lots of balls in the rotating bin, it is helpful to look at a real world situation, but one where the actual investment under consideration has had only two years of returns, and it is these two actual historical rates that get written on the balls, which are then dropped into the rotating bin.

The prudent investing couple Dave and Deana from Denver have just such an illustration. They bought several shares of a given stock at the beginning of Year 1 at $100 per share. During the course of Year 1, they watched with glee as the stock rose in value to $171.80 per share – a 71.8% increase. This increase is, of course, the product of many market forces. It could have been due to superior management of the company, a big unanticipated sale, or just plain market exuberance, which occurs from time to time.

They decided to hold the shares for one more year. However, the fortunes of Year 1 did not repeat. At the end of Year

2 each share was only worth $100 – the same value that Dave and Deana initially paid. Rats! Note again that while it took a 71.8% increase to get the original share price of $100 up to the $171.80 level, it only takes a 41.8% decrease to bring this higher share price back to its original starting point. This is because the 71.8% increase occurs when the share has a relatively low value, $100, and the 41.8% decrease occurs when the share has a relatively high value, $171.80.

Negative returns tend to have a bigger dollar impact than the same level of positive returns because they occur when the market is at a relative high. Separating rates of return from the actual market conditions that created them, and then treating positive and negative returns as equally likely to occur, is a process that tends to overstate the effect of the positive return, and understate the effect of the negative return. Yet it is exactly these two rates, the -41.8% and the 71.8%, that get written on the two balls in our two-ball rotating bin example. Dave and Deana may then use this rotating bin to model future anticipated investment results from this particular investment.

But Dave and Deana have some concerns. To illustrate this point, they wonder if they should be congratulating themselves on having achieved a 15% arithmetic mean return on their two-year investment or bemoaning the fact that they didn't make any money. If they think about holding the stock for another two years, they are less inclined to think that they would get a 15% return for each year, and more inclined to think that the stock price might stay around the $100 level.

In either case, they are trying to extrapolate the future based on "reading the tea leaves" of actual market behavior. If they treat the two events, the 71.8% gain and the 41.8% loss, as completely unrelated – one event had nothing to do with the other: no market correction, no profit taking, etc. – they recognize that they are following the ideas of modern finance. On the other hand, as they sit and discuss the future of this investment, they are somewhat inclined to link the two events and recognize that the superior performance of Year 1 may have had an impact on the negative performance of Year 2.

Their line of thinking is as follows. They recognize that the market in its infinite wisdom is the ultimate decider of an appropriate share value. If the share value grows too high, the market will bring it back down. If the share value drops too low, the market will bring it back up. Continuing with this thought but being mindful of the history of their actual investment, Dave and Deana suspect that the wisdom of the market might be that this particular share should sell for around $100.

The year that the share price went up to $171.80 needed some correcting, and the market brought it back to $100 with a 41.8% loss. If the share price had first dropped by 41.8% from $100 to $58.20, the market correction would be in the opposite direction. But it would take a 71.8% positive return to bring the share back to the $100 level - the appropriate share price all along. This "return to the original starting point" only requires a 41.8% loss to offset a 71.8% gain no matter which event comes first. Dave and Deana consider this to be a reasonable possibility, and they are becoming a little more leery of the modern finance concept of using the large rotating bin filled with actual historical rate of return results as a realistic forecasting tool.

To drive this point home, it is entertaining to consider one last two-rate example. In this case a start-up software company went out like gangbusters. Initial marketing efforts were fantastic, and the company had a long and impressive list of potential customers ready to purchase the new software. The company had a 130% return for its first year. The original share price of $100 climbed all the way to $230. The CEO of the company, the CFO of the company, and all the stockholders were delighted.

But in the second year, the bottom fell out. The software products that had been promised to the public didn't work, and other firms were able to produce products that did work. It was decided that there was no way that this company could succeed and the company went out of business. Of course the share price fell to $0. Thus, in the second year the company stock experienced a 100% loss. Every single investor lost his or her entire investment.

Now consider the modern finance model for the expected return on shares of stock in this company. The model places both of the known rates of return, the 130% gain and the 100% loss, into a giant rotating bin and concludes that in the future, the stock in this company will have a 15% best estimate rate of return. To many people this would seem to be a surprising conclusion. After all, the company that produced these two rates of return which are now in the rotating bin is now kaput. Most people would conclude that the best estimate rate of return for shares of stock in a company that is now out of business is probably zero.

LARGER ROTATING BINS OF ACTUAL DATA

The above paragraphs used simple data illustrations to discuss the theory behind selecting the arithmetic mean as a best estimate forecasting tool and showed some of the problems with this approach when one has only two data elements. While you might think that these problems disappear when using larger data sets, such is not the case. When using a much more detailed actual historical data set, there is still the problem of selecting appropriate data from the historical record in order to generate rates of return, which in turn may be written on the balls that get tossed into the giant rotating bin.

As shown in Chapter 3, the data that would be obtained by using one fiscal year end can be significantly different from the data obtained by using a different fiscal year end. The results from the rotating bin model using one set of fiscal year end data will be very different from the results obtained from a rotating bin model that uses data from a different fiscal year. Yet there is no real reason to pick one fiscal year over any other. Finally, it needs to be pointed out that the basic concept of using the rotating bin always forecasts a long-term wealth that is significantly larger than the actual long-term wealth that provides the data.

For example, using the *SBBI Yearbook* information for large company stock returns from each calendar year, a giant rotating bin based on 82 different annual results may be created. However, when one uses this bin to make forecasts, the expected ending wealth (how much money you will have after 82 years) becomes $13,136. This number is derived in exactly the same manner as the average ending wealth in the simple two-rate models shown above. It was obtained by taking the average of all the possible 82-year results. Yet this number is more than four times the wealth actually achieved by the original data of $3,246.

This important point may not be understood by many of the users of modern finance techniques, so it bears repeating one more time. Even though the actual wealth generated over the 82-year period by the Ibbotson data was $3,246, the common forecasting model created from this data has an average ending wealth at the end of 82 years of $13,136. Investors using this model are making decisions based on the assumption that the expected value of future 82-year wealth will be significantly larger than the wealth that was actually observed. This point seems to indicate that there is a fundamental problem with taking actual historical results and dropping them into a giant rotating bin as a tool for making forecasts.

To further demonstrate the problem, consider a long-term forecast made from a second rotating bin that also has 82 balls. The same Ibbotson large company stock return data will be used; however, this time the annual rates will be determined using a fiscal year that runs from July 1 to June 30. There are 81 natural such fiscal years in the Ibbotson data, and the 82nd year can be made by combining the short periods from 1926 and 2007. Using this rotating bin model, the expected ending wealth becomes $27,980. This number is more than 8 times the original ending wealth that serves as the source for the data.

The conceptual result using the 82 annual returns is no different than was the case with the simple model using only two returns: the -41.8% and the 71.8%. Although Dave and Deana made no money at all on their actual investment, modern finance would like them to believe that if they invested the same way year after year, on average their two-year investment would not end with a $100 share price, but would end with a $132.25 share price. The ending two-year wealth produced by the modern finance model is significantly larger than the actual two-year wealth earned by Dave and Deana. But this extra anticipated gain is all based on the assumption that Dave and Deana might see two good years, 71.8% years, come back to back.

The model used in modern finance is based on the concept that the good and bad years may be treated as having no impact on one another. The investors who made buy and sell decisions on the stock that produced the -41.8% in Year 2 were not being affected by the fact that the stock had earned 71.8% in the prior year. Modern finance treats these two results as independent events. However, when one factors in the realities of the market place, this conclusion may not be the best.

The creation of rotating bins in the manner described above will always produce expected ending wealth that exceeds the actual history that serves as the source for the data. In some cases these excess results can be quite significant, even if the size of the data sample remains constant. As noted above, using a rotating bin with 82 balls that reflect returns based on calendar years for the Ibbotson large company stock return data yields a model with expected 82-year wealth of $13,136. However, using the identical data, but changing the measurement period to fiscal years ending June 30 of each year still produces a rotating bin model with 82 balls in it. However, in this case the expected 82-year wealth becomes $27,980. Yet both of these models were derived from the same data – the one with actual ending 82-year wealth of only $3,246.

As if these numbers weren't bad enough, consider the case of Ibbotson small company stock data. The actual ending wealth that serves as the source for the data is $15,091.10. If one makes a rotating bin model using the 82 calendar years of data, the expected ending wealth becomes, gulp, $412,651. As bad as this number is, if the model were changed so that the 82 years of data are for fiscal years ending March 31 instead of calendar years, the new rotating bin model expected wealth becomes, gulp, gulp, gulp, $1,992,685!

This number is obtained in exactly the same way that was used for the simple little two-ball rotating bin illustrations. It is just the average of all the possible ending wealth values for the model. This average wealth of $1,992,685 seems to be a bit unusual, given that the actual ending wealth that serves as the source for the data is only $15,091.10. Investors using a computer software product that seems to be encouraging them to achieve greater investment returns by investing in the stocks of smaller companies may want to keep this illustration in mind.

No matter how good the actual history was, the rotating bin model will always predict higher levels of expected wealth in the future. To many people, this outlook of continued rate of return improvement is just too rosy an outlook. This is especially true when one compares the huge levels of expected long-term wealth derived from the model with the actual long-term wealth that serves as the source for the data.

THE ARITHMETIC MEAN PHILOSOPHY

Arithmetic-mean based forecast models, which are common in modern finance, are based on a philosophy that each observed historical return, whether it is a monthly, quarterly, or annual return, constitutes an independently determined result. The results that preceded any given rate of return had absolutely no bearing on the most recent rate. When a model is created using this assumption, the model always forecasts a larger expected ending wealth than what was actually observed.

Previously, the factors of market correction, price/earnings ratios, bubbles, irrational market exuberance, and the fact that it only takes a 41.8% decrease to offset a 71.8% increase have all been cited as reasons for not adopting the assumption that each year's return is an independent event. However, there is another, perhaps even stronger reason, and it is presented as follows.

Imagine that you are in a large auditorium, and up on the left-hand side of stage the certified representative of a major accounting firm is going to provide you with the estimated value of $1.00 if it is invested for 82 years. He does this by drawing 984 balls out of a giant rotating bin of monthly results. After each individual drawing he dutifully notes the value on the ball that was drawn, and then he replaces the ball in the bin before the next drawing. He also compounds these results to make the announcement that the independently determined 82-year wealth based on monthly drawings is $3,246.39. The audience claps respectfully to thank him for his efforts. He takes a small bow.

On the right-hand side of the stage a different certified representative of a major accounting firm is also going to provide you with the estimated value of $1.00 if it is invested for 82 years. However, he does this by drawing 82 balls out of a giant rotating bin of yearly results. After each individual drawing he dutifully notes the value on each ball, and then replaces the ball in the bin before the next drawing. He compounds his results to make the announcement that the independently determined 82-year wealth based on annual drawings is $3,246.39. Now the audience gasps. If you were in the audience, you would probably think that something was pretty fishy here!

It is statistically impossible that these two independent determinations would yield the same ending wealth. Yet this is what happens when modern finance extracts data from a single historical record. Clearly, the annual, quarterly, or monthly historical results are just the periodic observations of a single 82-year wealth accumulation. The mathematical theory of probability and statistics would suggest that this single observation of wealth should become the average of all the possibilities for 82-year wealth in the rotating bin model. In the current modern finance models the actually observed wealth is always below the anticipated model wealth. And as shown above, sometimes the actual historical wealth is below the anticipated model wealth by outrageously significant amounts.

INVESTOR IMPACT

There are geometric-mean-based forecast models where the expected long-term wealth of the model matches the actual long-term wealth of the historical data. For example, such a model will provide investors with information assuming that an investment in large company stocks, such as those included in the Ibbotson data, have an expected 82-year wealth of $3,246, the actually observed number, and not the high number of $13,136. These models will provide investors with information that is not based on the unrealistic assumption that the future will be significantly better than the past.

Table 13 below shows the impact that the change from an arithmetic-mean-based forecasting philosophy to a geo-metric-mean-based forecasting philosophy would have on the information provided to an average investor. A change to geo-metric-based forecasting might cause either a change in investment strategy, or even more likely, a change in the amount an investor chooses to save for retirement or other purpose. In short, the common use of an arithmetic mean of historical data as a "best estimate" of future investment returns provides the average investor with an inaccurate, and overstated, expectation of gain.

Table 13

A COMPARISON OF PROJECTED
LARGE COMPANY STOCK RETURNS

Percentile	Geometric Annual Return	Arithmetic Annual Return
90.0%	34.23%	38.64%
75.0	21.57	24.53
60.0	13.49	15.59
50.0	8.89	10.52
40.0	4.48	5.67
25.0	(2.46)	(1.92)
10.0	(11.66)	(11.90)
Expected Value	10.36%	12.26%

As a second comparison, consider the possible 20-year values of a $10,000 investment. At the 50th percentile, using geometric methods, the investment is expected to be worth $55,000; however, using arithmetic methods, the investment is expected to be worth $73,900. At the 25th percentile the two expected wealth values are $33,500 and $43,300. At the 75th percentile the two expected wealth values are $90,100 and $126,000. Clearly, the change in forecasting approach has a material impact on information that would be provided any given investor.

The Statistical Analyst's Workshop

Chapter 5

MYTH 3: THE LOGNORMAL PROBABILITY DENSITY FUNCTION PROVIDES A REASONABLE DISTRIBUTION BASIS FOR HISTORICAL INVESTMENT RETURN RESULTS

Boatloads of data make some folks quite queasy.

Allergic to numbers? You might even get sneezy.

But just the right tool

yields charts that are cool.

A well-stocked work shop makes a hard task now easy.

MYTH 3: THE LOGNORMAL PROBABILITY DENSITY FUNCTION PROVIDES A REASONABLE DISTRIBUTION BASIS FOR HISTORICAL INVESTMENT RETURN RESULTS

Myth 3 introduces some heavy duty mathematical terminology, which makes busting it more of a challenge. Yet Myth 3 is probably the most important myth to be busted in this book. This is because the assumption that Myth 3 is true drives virtually all of the key results of modern finance, including various results provided to everyday investors. The implications of this myth-busting chapter are rather far-reaching. The challenge of this chapter is to provide enough visual imagery that everyday investors will be able to see exactly what Myth 3 is saying and exactly why Myth 3 is not true.

The first step in this process will be to explain and illustrate the role of a probability density function. A probability density function is nothing more than a mathematical formula that may be used to describe how some data is distributed. Recall that Charts 1, 2, and 3 all showed the distribution of data. Chart 1 showed the distribution of historical monthly rates of return earned on investments made in large company stocks, Chart 2 showed the distribution of historical monthly rates of return earned on investments made in small company stocks, and Chart 3 dealt with the distribution of the number of heads that would be seen if 20 coins were tossed into the air.

In each case these charts were then used to answer some percentage chance questions. In the case of Charts 1 and 2, the percentage chance questions had to do with anticipated future investment results. For example, what is the percentage chance that for a given month the rate of return seen on a large company stock investment might exceed 5.8%? In the case of Chart 3 the percentage chance question might be what is the percentage chance of seeing 9 heads if 20 coins were tossed into the air?

In each case the percentage chance questions were answered by direct reference to the respective chart. If the chart could be replaced by a mathematical formula, then lots of different percentage chance questions could be easily answered by using the new formula. You would not be restricted to only being able to answer questions that could be answered by the specific chart. Myth 3 deals with the assumption made by modern finance that a very specific mathematical formula accurately describes historical investment return distributions, such as those shown in Charts 1 and 2. This specific mathematical formula is called the "lognormal probability density function."

The dramatic demonstration provided in this chapter to bust Myth 3 will be relatively straight forward. It will be to show that this particular mathematical formula, the lognormal probability density function, is the wrong probability density function to describe the distribution of historical investment returns as shown in Charts 1 and 2. This will be done in two steps. The first step will be to demonstrate a relatively poor match between the actually observed distributions of historical returns and distributions that are predicted by the lognormal probability density function. The second step will be to show that another mathematical formula, the conditional lognormal probability density function, does a much better job of providing distributions of results that match the distributions of actual historical data.

As background for the busting of Myth 3, it is first necessary to describe probability density functions and the role that they play in making forecasts. This challenge will be met by first turning once more to the coin flipping illustration shown in Chart 3.

COIN FLIPPING REVISITED

To gain an understanding for what Myth 3 is saying and an understanding of probability density functions in general, it is helpful to revisit Chart 3. The information presented in Chart 3 was obtained when a researcher actually took 20 coins and a clip board into the lab and began the coin flipping data gathering process. On the first toss of 20 coins, the researcher counted that there were 7 heads. The researcher put a check mark beside the "7" on the clip board, gathered up the coins, and proceeded to do the second toss. This time the toss resulted in 11 heads. The researcher put a check mark beside the "11" on the clip board, gathered up the coins, and proceeded to do the third toss. The process was continued until the 20 coins had been tossed 984 times. The entire process took about ten hours.

The results of this specific experiment are the data that is shown in Chart 3. Of course, a second researcher could have completed the same experiment in a second lab room. He or she would have come up with a different distribution of the number of heads, but because we are dealing with coin flips, there is a general sense that the second researcher would have come up with a distribution somewhat similar to what is shown in Chart 3. Had a government grant been available, the entire process probably could have involved a dozen researchers just to make sure that the data gathering exercise was as complete as possible.

However, instead of using any researchers, Chart 3 could have been developed without ever flipping a single coin. Using the mathematics of probability, it is possible to derive a mathematical formula, called the binomial probability density function, that would have provided a very reasonable distribution of the number of heads that one would expect to see if he or she actually did the 20-coin toss experiment 984 times. The exact formula for the binomial probability density function is not particularly relevant. What is important is to know that this particular mathematical formula exists, and that it does a good job of matching the data distribution as shown in Chart 3.

Chart 7 is used to compare the results from the actual coin tossing experiment as shown in Chart 3 with what would have been predicted using the binomial probability density function. As seen from Chart 7, the match between the actual results and the predicted results is pretty close. For example, in the actual experiment 117 of the 984 tosses had 12 heads. The estimate obtained from using the binomial probability density function is that 118 of the 984 tosses would have 12 heads. In the actual experiment 160 of the tosses had 9 heads; the binomial probability density function estimate called for 158 of the tosses to have 9 heads. While other comparisons are not quite this close, all things considered the match seems to be pretty good. Really, really interested readers are welcome to do their own experiments.

Chart 7

COIN FLIPPING EXPERIMENT WITH 20 COINS

COMPARISON OF DISTRIBUTION FOR THE NUMBER OF HEADS OUT OF 984 TRIALS OF THE EXPERIMENT WITH EXPECTED BINOMIAL DISTRIBUTION

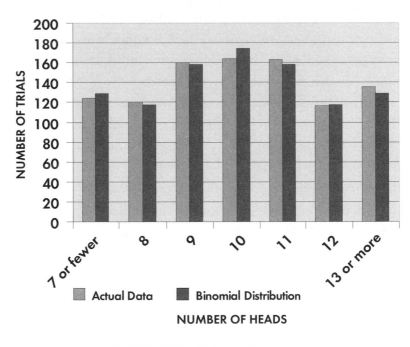

The advantage to having an accurate probability density function is that once such a formula is identified, this mathematical formula may be used to answer percentage chance questions, such as those illustrated above, instead of referring to a chart such as Chart 3. Having a probability density function available makes it possible to answer many more percentage chance questions than if one only is able to use a chart that has limited values.

While Chart 3 dealt with the distribution of coin flips, Charts 1 and 2 concern the distribution of actually observed rates of investment return. Although the three charts look somewhat similar, there are two key differences between Charts 1 and 2 and Chart 3. The first difference is the amount of time it took to gather the data, which is displayed in the chart. For the coin-flipping chart, it took about 10 hours to repeat the experiment 984 times and to tabulate the results. For the two investment return charts, it took 82 years to gather the data! That's a lot of time to gather only 984 pieces of information.

This point underscores another critical issue. With coin flips, the experiment can be repeated many times just to confirm that actual distributions do in fact come close to matching the distribution that is predicted by the binomial probability density function. With investment returns, there will only be the one history. It takes so long to gather data, it is not possible to have repeated actual tests to see if the prediction described by a given probability density function is accurate or not.

The second difference is that the density function which reasonably describes the coin-tossing data as shown in Chart 3 was developed directly from the mathematical principles of probability. This is not possible for Charts 1 and 2 as there is no mathematical theory of probability that is appropriate for estimating the distribution for investment returns.

Even though no such theory exists, for lots of practical reasons, not the least of which is the amount of time it takes to gather data, it is highly desirable to also have a probability density function that would reasonably describe the distribution of investment return results as shown in Charts 1 and 2 in the same way that the binomial probability density function may be used to describe the distribution of coin flips in Chart 3.

Modern finance has assumed that a probability density function, known as the lognormal probability density function, provides reasonable estimates for the distribution of historical investment returns. This means that percentage chance questions may be answered using this mathematical formula, rather than referring to the limited values such as those that are shown in Charts 1 and 2. The section below discusses the process involved in picking such a probability density function when no mathematical theory of probability is available.

THE STATISTICAL ANALYST

The task of finding a probability density function that reflects the data in Chart 1 or Chart 2 is more difficult than finding a probability density function appropriate for Chart 3. This is because the coin flipping exercise may be completely and fully analyzed using the mathematics of probability, whereas there is no corresponding mathematics of probability associated with investment returns. However, even though the mathematics of probability is not available, it is still possible to develop reasonable probability density functions to describe actual data distributions. The task of deciding which probability density function is the "right" probability density function is the task of the statistical analyst.

To better understand the role of the statistical analyst, I stopped by the workshop of Stu Stevens, Statistical Analyst. Stu's workshop is located near my house, and he was glad to have me stop by. There was a little bell on his workshop door that greeted visitors, and also let Stu know that he had company. There was a wood stove in the corner of his workshop. On the chilly day that I visited Stu, the wood stove provided gentle warmth for the entire place. I was curious about the process that Stu used to develop probability density functions when the mathematics of probability was not available.

Stu let me know that the statistical analyst has many tools in his workshop to help him try to make a good match between the distribution of the observed data and a proposed distribution of data as described by the probability density function. This is true even when the mathematics of probability is not available. He also indicated that in most situations the match between the distribution of the actual data and the distribution developed from the probability density function should be pretty good. There are just too many options available not to have a pretty good match.

Stu said that he would usually try to find out as much about the source of the data as possible, as there are several different approaches in conducting the search for a probability density function. For example, if the data has a definite starting point but no ending point, Stu said that he might first turn to a general probability density function known as the Poisson probability density function as he begins his assignment.

As an example of data that has a definite starting point but no fixed ending point, consider the number of strokes that it takes to complete a given hole on a golf course. The starting point is one stroke. It will take at least one stroke to complete the hole. If this happens, you will be extremely happy, and not give a hoot about the probability density function associated with the number of strokes that it takes to complete a particular hole.

You would probably be almost as happy if you could complete the hole in 2 or 3 strokes. For many golfers the most common number of strokes will be between 4 and 7. Finally, I know from personal experience that there really is no number of strokes that will serve as a fixed ending point. If one had an accurate probability density function describing the number of strokes that it would take to complete a certain golf hole, then one could answer percentage chance questions such as what is the percentage chance that the hole could be completed in 5 strokes.

This illustration serves a second purpose. Knowing the answer to a percentage chance question, such as the number of strokes it takes for a group of golfers to complete a given hole, may not provide relevant information for the particular golfer. Clearly Tiger Woods contributes to the data showing a low number of strokes, whereas I contribute data showing a high number of strokes.

As a second example, Stu noted that if the data appears to be somewhat uniformly distributed about a given central value, he might start searching for a good match by using a probability density function that is known as the normal probability density function. This is the probability density function that describes the standard bell-shaped curve that you may be familiar with. Continuing with this particular example, Stu had an illustration showing a "typical" distribution that might be reasonably described by the normal probability density function. In other words, if the distribution of the actual data looked like the distribution of the data in the illustration below, there exists a mathematical formula that could be used to describe the distribution. This formula could be used to answer percentage chance questions instead of referring to charts such as Chart 1 or Chart 2.

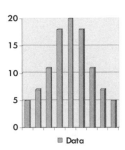

While this might be the starting point, Stu pointed out a special vise he can clamp onto the bell-shaped curve. By using the vise, he could build a mathematical formula that would yield a distribution that is somewhat taller and skinnier than the standard shape. On the other hand, he also has a special press that he could use to build a mathematical formula that would describe a distribution that is shorter and flatter. After applying the special vise, the bell-shaped curve may look like the illustration on the left below. After applying the special press, the bell-shaped curve may look like the illustration on the right below.

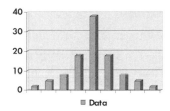 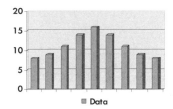

The critical point once again is that if a particular distribution is similar to the patterns shown above, there exists a probability density function which could be used to answer percentage chance questions. One would not be restricted to only answering questions based on the specific data shown in a given chart.

Stu was quite candid in pointing out that the statistical analyst faces lots of interesting challenges. In particular, he has special shaping tools to alter the formula such that the distribution produced by the formula either tilts a little to the right to satisfy Republicans or a little to the left to satisfy Democrats. Two illustrations of this "tilting" exercise are shown below. Again, keep in mind that for each of the illustrations shown below there is a mathematical formula that may be used to describe the indicated distribution.

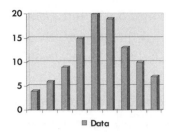

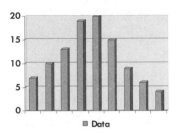

In short, Stu noted that the statistical analyst has lots of tools to use in trying to come up with a mathematical formula that can then be used to describe the distribution of data that comes from an actual observation and that there are literally an infinite number of possibilities for a probability density function designed to provide a distribution that matches the actual distribution of any particular set of data. Stu reiterated that given the wealth of resources available to the statistical analyst, any reasonable probability density function should provide for a pretty good match to the actual data. I thanked Stu for his time and the tour of his workshop, and then went back to work on this book.

THE LOGNORMAL PROBABILITY DENSITY FUNCTION

It has been common in modern finance to assume that the distribution of investment return results can be reasonably described by using a general mathematical formula known as the lognormal probability density function. The specific lognormal probability density function illustrated in this book is the one described on pages 162-163 of the *SBBI Yearbook*.

The first step in busting Myth 3 is to show that the lognormal probability density function mentioned above yields distributions that do a poor job of matching the actual historical data. Chart 1 showed the distribution of 984 actual large stock monthly returns from the Ibbotson data. Chart 8 shows this same data from Chart 1, but it also includes the distribution of 984 rates of return if they were distributed according to the lognormal probability density function as described in the *SBBI Yearbook*.

Chart 8

DISTRIBUTION OF MONTHLY LARGE COMPANY STOCK RETURNS COMPARED WITH LOGNORMAL ASSUMPTION

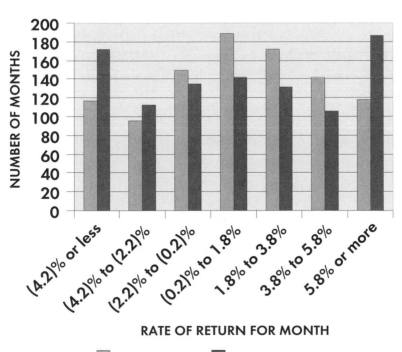

The comparison is a bit surprising given the wide spread use of the lognormal probability density function assumption. It is clear that the lognormal probability density function predicts a much broader distribution of results than what is supported by the actual data. It predicts many more months with very large returns and many more months with very low returns (this means returns that are big negative numbers) than what has been actually observed. In short it does not seem to be providing a reasonable basis for describing the distribution of actual historical data.

To emphasize this point, consider just this one specific comparison. The actual large company stock rate of return data shows that only 118 months had rates of return that were more than 5.8%. The lognormal probability density function estimates that 186 months would have a rate of return that is more than 5.8%. Thus, using the data, you might expect that the percentage chance of achieving a 5.8% or larger rate of return for a given month is 118/984 or 12%. However, the commonly used lognormal density function raises this percentage to 186/984 or 19%.

I ran this exact illustration by Stu Stevens, and he was just as concerned as I was. He reemphasized the point that with all the tools available to a statistical analyst, it should be possible to get a much better match than the one that was currently being advocated by modern finance. He asked me to point out to readers that the next time they might be using a sophisticated computer program that is encouraging them to invest more in large company stocks because they are likely to see a higher rate of return, they might want to keep this illustration in mind. The sophisticated computer program may be based on a lognormal density function that is assuming that there 19% chance of earning a monthly rate of return that is greater than 5.8%, when the actual history shows that a monthly rate this high has only occurred 12% of the time.

As a second comparison, Chart 9 shows the distribution of the 984 monthly small company stock returns that were originally presented in Chart 2, but it also includes the distribution of 984 returns assuming that these returns were distributed according to the *SBBI Yearbook* lognormal probability density function. Again the match seems relatively poor, and the lognormal probability density function is developing a distribution that is much wider than what is supported by the actual data itself.

Chart 9

DISTRIBUTION OF MONTHLY SMALL COMPANY STOCK RETURNS COMPARED WITH LOGNORMAL ASSUMPTION

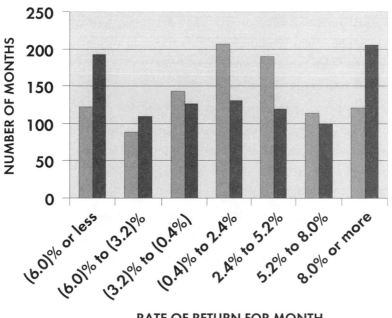

Furthermore, in each of the above cases the particular log-normal probability density function was selected as it has been offered by modern finance as the appropriate tool for describing actual investment returns. If the fit is so poor, maybe the answer is to consider a different probability density function.

CONDITIONAL LOGNORMAL PROBABILITY DENSITY FUNCTION

It is one thing to show that the lognormal probability density function does a poor job of matching the data, but in order to bust Myth 3 it is necessary to show that another type of probability density function would work much better. This new candidate is known as the conditional lognormal probability density function. Yes, that is a lot of words to describe a mathematical formula, but this formula yields much better results. The rationale for its use and the demonstration of the better results are shown below.

Investment returns are not determined by drawing balls out of rotating bins or by flipping coins. They are determined by actual investors on an almost continuous basis. As noted before, when Allen in Altoona decides to pay $20.00 for a share of a given stock, that transaction sets the price at $20.00. The price is changed when Bob in Boston enters into a transaction a few seconds later at $20.50 per share. This then becomes the new price until Cheryl in Chicago executes at trade at $20.25. These transactions give rise to changes in share value which eventually become calculated rates of return.

Also, it is pretty clear that Bob in Boston did not know what Allen in Altoona had paid for his shares of stock, and that Cheryl in Chicago didn't know what either of them had paid for their shares of stock. However, after the passage of enough time (one day, a few hours?), it is clear that that Mike in Minneapolis is aware of the prices paid by Allen, Bob, and Cheryl. Recent histories of changes in stock price are readily available to all investors, and it is pretty clear that the investors use this information when making investment decisions. All of this would argue that Mike in Minneapolis is not making an "independent" decision, in the sense of drawing a ball out of giant rotating bin, but is "conditioning" his decision based on recent market activity.

This understanding of the underlying source of investment returns is critical, as it argues that if one is trying to select a probability density function to describe the distribution of historical investment returns, it might be better to look at one of the probability density functions associated with conditional probability distributions. In short, instead of using the general lognormal probability density function illustrated above, which is appropriate for independently determined data, it might be a better idea to use a probability density function that is more appropriate for data that is conditional in nature.

Given the ultimate source of investment return data, that being the individual decisions made by investors, and given that this data seems to be conditional in nature it appears to make more sense to describe the distribution of investment returns using a probability density function that reflects these realities of the stock market. The conditional lognormal probability density function turns out to work much better at describing a distribution of investment returns, which is much closer to matching actual historical data. For the curious, this probability density function along with a more complete mathematical description of both the lognormal and conditional lognormal probability density functions is shown in Appendix 2. If you are thinking of looking at Appendix 2 to see the formula, be forewarned. This formula is ugly! The typist who put this book together for me deserves five gold stars just for getting all the right letters in all the right spots.

But in probability density functions, it is not simplicity or beauty that counts, but how accurate the formula is in describing the distribution of the observed data. The conditional lognormal probability density function is way more complex than and not nearly as pretty as the lognormal density function. However, when reasonable parameters are selected for this new probability density function, and the resulting conditional lognormal distribution is compared with actual data, there is a significant improvement in the match over what was shown above.

Chart 10 compares the distribution of the Ibbotson large company stock rate of return data with the distribution assuming the data was distributed according to the conditional lognormal probability density function, and Chart 11 makes the same comparison for the Ibbotson small company stock rate of return data. Both of these charts indicate a much closer match than what was obtained using the lognormal probability density function as described in the *SBBI Yearbook*.

Chart 10

DISTRIBUTION OF MONTHLY LARGE COMPANY STOCK RETURNS COMPARED WITH CONDITIONAL LOGNORMAL ASSUMPTION

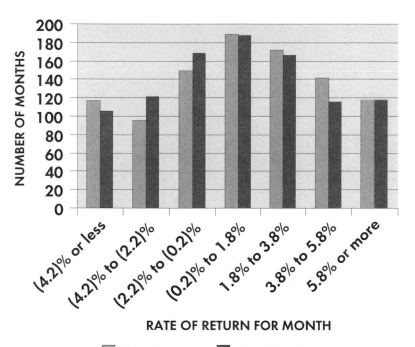

RATE OF RETURN FOR MONTH

☐ Actual Data   ■ Conditional Lognormal

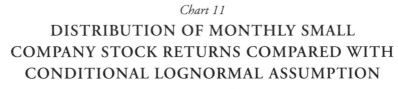

Chart 11

DISTRIBUTION OF MONTHLY SMALL COMPANY STOCK RETURNS COMPARED WITH CONDITIONAL LOGNORMAL ASSUMPTION

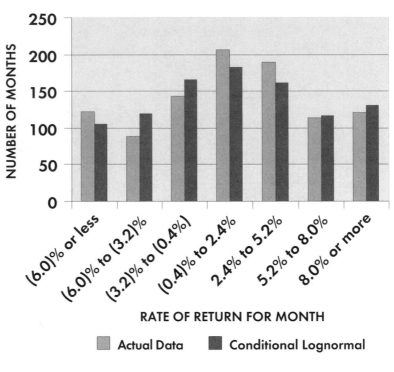

The modern finance selection of the lognormal probability density function is based on the assumption that each observed historical return may be treated as if it were an independently determined event. This would be reasonable if the investors who are making decisions about any given share price did not take recent market activity into account when making their decisions to enter into an actual transaction.

However, when one reflects on normal stock market operations, it seems to indicate that investors are keenly aware of market history. Terms like market correction, bottoming out, rebounding, profit-taking, and price/earnings ratios at historical highs or lows all reflect the fact that investors are very aware of market conditions that affect their investment decisions. This line of reasoning argues strongly for the use of a conditional lognormal probability density function. The actual comparison of the two different candidates, by comparing Chart 8 with Chart 10 and comparing Chart 9 with Chart 11, does not leave much room for doubt.

INVESTOR IMPACT

All of the first three myths have been busted by reflecting the same market reality. That reality is that observed market rates of return are not independently determined events. Instead, observed market rates of return are very clearly periodic measures of the change in wealth of a single long-term investment history. For statistical analysis purposes these periodic measures are all conditional events. Any periodic measure, daily, weekly, monthly or annually, only reflects the same single history. The change from the independent assumption to the conditional assumption is very significant and far-reaching.

The year 2008 saw a huge amount of turmoil in the financial services industry. Bear Stearns went out of business, as did Lehman Brothers Holdings. AIG, the insurance giant, needed a significant guarantee. Finally, the Congress of the United States approved a $700 billion bailout of the financial services industry.

Many of the general news articles dealing with the above problems refer to inaccurately priced risk. There is the possibility that the assessment of risk in these situations is following in the pattern set by modern finance investment return forecasting. That pattern is to treat historical data as if it were a set of independently determined events, when a more complete analysis would indicate that the data is conditional in nature.

If data is conditional in nature, then the treatment of it as independent data will yield inaccurate results. The difference between Chart 8 and Chart 10, or the difference between Chart 9 and Chart 11, is clear. At least with regard to investment returns, conditional data is being treated in an inappropriate fashion. Perhaps the same problem is occurring in other risk assessment situations as well and is contributing significantly to the problems seen in the financial services industry in 2008.

Risky Rick and His Cat, Rex, Ponder Option Investing

Chapter 6

STOCK OPTIONS AND STOCK OPTION PRICING

Stock option investing is as hard as it gets.

To buy one share of stock, or make ten little bets.

The cost is the same; the payoff is not,

possibly ranging from oodles to naught.

Do ponder wisely; get help from your pets.

Stock option investing is as hard as it gets.

INTRODUCTION

The first three myths in this book involved general history-based forecasting issues in modern finance. The myth busting showed the difficulties in calculating an arithmetic mean from historical data and the impossibility of using an arithmetic mean of historical data as a reasonable forecasting tool. The busting of Myth 3 showed the greater accuracy of using the conditional lognormal probability density function instead of the basic lognormal probability density function when trying to model historical investment returns.

The problem in each case is attributed to the assumption, common in modern finance, that each observed historical investment return constitutes an independently determined data element. While the demonstration involving the numerous arithmetic means could have been completed at any time, it took several years in order to accumulate the data necessary to demonstrate the problems with the expected distribution of monthly returns. This time delay to gather the necessary data has certainly been a significant hurdle in the recognition of problems in modern finance. But now that sufficient history is available, the move from the "independent" assumption to the "conditional" assumption needs to be made.

The assumption of independent historical data also affects all areas of modern finance, not just investment forecasts. The move from the independent assumption to the conditional assumption will play a big role in these areas as well. In particular, the move from the independent assumption to the conditional assumption has a significant impact on the pricing of stock options and other sophisticated investments known generally as derivatives. The next three myths to be busted in this book all involve stock options and the pricing of stock options.

Since some readers of this book may not be familiar with stock options, this chapter provides a very brief primer. This primer is designed to clearly illustrate certain key aspects of stock option contracts. The information provided here will cover the basics of two very simple stock option contracts: a European-style stock call option contract and a European-style stock put option contract. In addition, this chapter provides some general background for a very well-known stock option pricing model: The Black-Scholes Stock Option Pricing Model.

But before getting all bogged down in stock options and pricing models, let's catch up with our friends Dave and Deana from Denver. This time Dave and Deana are on a vacation to Churchill Downs in Louisville, Kentucky. Every now and then Dave and Deana have a little fun engaging in the sport of kings, horse racing!

HORSE RACING

Dave and Deana are as serious about their days at the horse races as they are about their investments. As per their usual custom, Dave and Deana decide to purchase a racing guide, which will provide them with detailed information about the horses that will be running that day. Using this guide, and any hot tips or other information, they decide which horse might win a given race and then decide whether or not to bet on that horse. Doing this kind of research is not unlike the research they do in deciding whether or not to make a particular stock investment. While most horse races have a variety of different bets that may be placed, for purposes of this illustration we will assume that Dave and Deana and other horse racing fans may only make bets that will provide for a payoff if the horse that they bet on actually wins the race.

After studying the information about the horses that are running, Dave and Deana select the horse that they think has the best chance of winning the race. In this illustration, that horse is Stock Option Baby, a 3-year old from Lexington, Kentucky. Then Dave goes to a wagering window at Churchill Downs and places a bet on Stock Option Baby. At the wagering window Dave spends $2 to get a small slip of paper that shows that the bet has been placed. Then they sit back to wait for the start of the race and the call of the announcer that: "The horses are in the starting gate and it's post time!" Like many fans, Dave and Deana get excited to watch the actual horse race unfold.

During the race itself, they yell and scream at Stock Option Baby to run as fast as he possibly can. They have a material interest in the outcome, for if Stock Option Baby wins, Dave and Deana will be able to take the small slip of paper back to the wagering window and exchange it for cash, perhaps as much as $10 or $20. This is a very handsome return for a $2 bet. If Stock Option Baby loses, they get to throw the little slip of paper into the garbage. This represents a 100% loss on the $2 bet. In horse racing, on any given race, the typical fan will either make a relatively nice return, or lose the entire wager.

It is interesting that many fans do yell for their favorite horse, yet it seems unlikely that this action actually makes the horse run any faster. However, if some of you believe this action does help, you may want to consider cheering for your favorite stock, once you have purchased a few shares of that stock, or (as will be shown below) if you have purchased a European-style stock call option on that stock. Who knows? It might help, and it couldn't hurt.

EUROPEAN-STYLE STOCK CALL
OPTION CONTACTS

The goal of *Six Myths in Modern Finance that Every Investor Needs to Know* is to create visual imagery that makes key mathematical concepts in modern finance more understandable to the average investor. Horse racing was presented as the opening section of this chapter for a specific reason. There are a lot of similarities between making a bet at the horse races and making an investment in a European-style stock call option contract.

The key points to keep in mind from the horse racing illustration are as follows: (1) The person who makes a bet at the horse races spends $2 to buy a piece of paper that has no value at the time it is purchased but may yield a sizeable return later. (2) This person needs to wait for a period of time, in this case the length of the horse race, in order to learn whether or not the piece of paper has value. (3) The cash payback to the person may be sizeable, but it often turns out to be zero, in which case the piece of paper may be discarded. This same three-step explanation is equally relevant for describing a European-style stock call option contract.

As defined in the modern finance literature, the general European-style stock call option is a formal contract that allows the holder of that contract to buy a particular share of stock at a fixed price on a specified date. However, in terms of financial impact to the investor who buys this stock call contract, the purchase of the contract is equivalent to making a "bet" on the future value of one share of the stock. The amount of the bet, or wager, is the price of the option contract. Once the bet is placed, the person making the bet needs to wait until a specific date, which is part of the contract. If on that date the share price of the underlying stock exceeds a given fixed number stated in the contract, called the strike price, the person making the bet will receive some money back. The payoff on the bet will be the difference between the actual market price of the stock on the specified date and the fixed strike price stated in the contract.

For example, assume that a simple one-year stock call option contract on Stock A with a strike price of $24 is available on January 5, 2009, and that this contract costs $2. This means that: (1) An investor can spend $2 on January 5, 2009, in order to place the bet. (2) The investor needs to wait for one year to the specific date of January 5, 2010, to learn whether or not the bet will generate any payoff. (3) If on January 5, 2010, the price of Stock A is greater than $24, then the bet will pay back the difference between the price of Stock A on that date and $24; if Stock A is selling for $24 or less on that date, the bet will pay back nothing.

When Dave or Deana want to collect on a bet that they made at the horse races, they only need to take the winning ticket back to the wagering window at the race track. Collecting on a winning stock call option bet is a bit more complicated, but the financial impact is exactly the same. In the example above if the actual share price on January 5, 2010, is $35, and the fixed strike price stated in the contract is $24, the person making the "bet" is entitled to an $11 payback, as this is the difference between $24 and $35.

Mechanically, the payback works as follows. The stock call contract permits the holder to purchase a share of Stock A for $24 on January 5, 2010. If the actual market price of Stock A on that day is $35, the holder will "exercise his option" under the contract to actually make the purchase of a share of Stock A at $24. But then he can turn around and sell this share for the current market value of $35, generating an $11 payoff on his investment in the contract. For purposes of this book, stock call option contracts will be treated as "bets" and the actual mechanics of cashing in a winning bet will not be emphasized.

As noted, purchasing a stock call option for $2 is like making a bet in a horse race for $2. In the horse race, you wind up cheering for your horse to finish first at the end of the race so that you can make money on your bet. In stock call options, you wind up cheering for the market price of your stock to exceed the strike price by the specified date so that you can make money on your stock call option investment.

The one-year period in the above example is referred to as the "term" of the contract. While some stock call option contracts (called American-style contracts) will allow the holder of the contract to take advantage of the contract's provisions at any time during the term of the contract, for purposes of all illustrations in this book, it will be assumed that the holder of the contract will only be able to take advantage of the contract's provisions on the last day of the contract's term. Thus, in the above illustration the holder of the stock call contract needs to wait the full year to see if he or she has made any money. These contracts are referred to as European-style option contracts.

If the share price on the last day of the term of the option exceeds the strike price, the payoff for the stock call option contract is determined as the difference between the share price on the last day of the term and the strike price. To further illustrate the example above; if the share price on January 5, 2010, is $30, the investor will receive $6 because the fixed strike price is $24. If the share price on January 5, 2010, is $40, the investor will receive $16 because the fixed strike price is still $24. Once the $2 bet is made on the future value of shares of Stock A, the investor really does have a reason to cheer for the stock to grow to levels well in excess of the strike price.

As a second illustration, consider a six-month stock call option on Stock B with a strike price of $50 per share, which is available on February 1, 2009, for a price of $3. If an investor decides to spend $3 to buy this stock call option on February 1, 2009, he needs to wait 6 months, the term of the contract, to see if he has made any money on his $3 bet. On August 1, 2009, if shares of Stock B are selling for $55, he will receive $5 for having made his $3 bet, by exercising his option to purchase a share for $50, and then selling it for $55. If on that date the shares of Stock B are selling for $65, he will receive $15 for having made his $3 bet, by exercising his option to purchase a share for $50, and then selling it for $65. However, if the shares of Stock B are selling for anything less than $50 on August 1, 2009, he will get nothing. In this case his option contract is like a losing ticket at a horse race. It just becomes waste paper to be discarded, and he will have spent his $3 for nothing.

The above explanation of stock call options has been simplified. Actual stock call options available on the open market are more complex. Yet the basic risk and reward characteristics of the simplified option described above are identical to the risk and reward characteristics of actual stock call options. Hence, the simplified version will work just fine for making any necessary illustrations in this book.

At first glance, a stock call option contract may seem to be somewhat of a strange investment. And it is. However, stock call option contracts do provide the possibility of great reward, but they also offer the potential for a significant loss. In short, they are very risky investments. Just to drive home the point one more time, buying stock call option contracts is not a whole lot different than making a bet on a horse such as Stock Option Baby. If you bet $2 on Stock Option Baby, and

Stock Option Baby actually wins the race, you have a great payoff. Ka-ching!! But if the horse finishes back in the pack, you lose your bet. Some bets payoff handsomely, and some bets pay off nothing!

At the race track, you study the past performance of various horses, decide which horse you think might win the race, place your $2 bet, wait for the race to be completed, and then, depending on the outcome of the race, either cash in your racing ticket, or toss it in the garbage. If the horse you pick wins the race, you wish you had made a bet that was larger than $2!

With stock call options, you study the past history of the underlying shares of stock, decide which shares of stock you think might grow to exceed the strike price (pick your horse), buy the option (place your bet), wait for the contract term to pass (watch the horse race), and either cash in your winning contract (winning ticket at the races) or toss it in the garbage. Notice that the garbage toss is identical in both situations.

THE RISK IN STOCK CALL OPTIONS VERSUS THE RISK IN STOCK INVESTMENTS

The following illustration will demonstrate just how risky stock call options can be. Assume that you have $20 to invest, and that you think that Stock A, which happens to be trading at $20 per share, looks like a good investment. You believe that the price of Stock A could increase in value to somewhere between $24 and $30 in one year's time. If you purchase a share of Stock A, and the share price grows from $20 to $24, you will have made a nice 20% return on your investment. The $4 gain divided by the initial $20 investment produces this 20% rate of return. Or if you purchase a share of Stock A, and the share price grows from $20 to $30, you will have made an even nicer 50% return on your investment. The $10 gain divided by the initial $20 investment produces this 50% rate of return. In either case, you will be kicking yourself for not having purchased more shares.

But now consider your choices if there is a one-year stock call option available on Stock A with a strike price of $24, and this stock call option contract is selling for $2. If you really, really, really believe that the share price might increase in value to $30, maybe it is wiser to buy 10 stock call options with your $20, rather than to purchase one share of stock. In this case you have spent $20 for a bet on the value of Stock A at a date one year in future. This is a bet, and if the price of Stock A on that date is less than $24 per share, you will lose your entire $20 bet. When you buy a stock call option, you own the bet; you do not own any shares of the stock. In horse racing, when you make the bet, you own the bet; you do not own the horse!

But if Stock A does rise in value to $30 per share at the end of the one-year option term, each of your options will be worth $6. This is the difference between the current market price of Stock A ($30) and the strike price of the option ($24). Your ten options (or bets) would produce a payoff for you of $60. You did not make a 50% return by buying one share of Stock A, you made a 200% return by buying the 10 options! Your original $20 investment turned into $60 cash. The $40 gain divided by the initial $20 investment produces the 200% return result.

That is the good news. Now consider the case where the stock only rises in value to $24 per share. In this case, your ten stock call options are not worth anything. In short, you have gotten nothing for your $20 that you spent on the 10 stock call option contracts. This translates into a complete loss of your $20, or a percentage loss of -100%.

If you thought investing in stocks entailed risk, try stock call options! In the illustration above, by purchasing one share of Stock A, your return would vary between 20% and 50% depending upon where in the range of $24 to $30 the final stock price falls. However, having the same range of final stock prices, $24 to $30, yields returns on the 10 stock call option contracts which range between -100%, if the stock only grows to $24 in value, to 200%, if the stock grows to $30 in value. The same behavior of the stock that generates a return range from 20% to 50% on an investment in the stock generates a return range from -100% to 200% on an investment in the options. Investing in stock call option contracts is not for those who are afraid of risks.

EUROPEAN-STYLE STOCK PUT OPTION CONTRACTS

It is possible to define a simplified stock put option contract that is similar in nature to the simplified stock call option contract defined above. The simplified stock put option contract has the identical risk and reward characteristics as traded European-style stock put option contracts and again serves the illustration purposes of this book quite well. As with the simplified stock call option contract, the purchaser of a stock put option contract is making a "bet" on the future value of a share of stock. However, in this case, the payoff only occurs when the share value of the stock is less than the strike price. The amount of payoff will be the fixed strike price less the actual share price on the last day of the term of the stock put option contract. To get this payoff using real stock put options, you might need to purchase the share at the current market value, and then turn around and sell it under the terms of the stock put contract.

Stock put options also have a horse racing analogy, just like stock call options. However, in this horse race the game is played a little differently than the normal horse race. In this race you decide which horse you think is going to lose the race. You then place your $2 bet on this horse, watch the race, and then cheer wildly as your horse falls to last in the field. For in this most unusual of horse racing bets, your bet pays off only when you correctly pick the losing horse! When buying a stock put option contract, you are rooting for the ending value of the share to be well below the strike price, somewhat like the losing horse in a horse race.

Continuing with the same illustration as above, assume that instead of thinking that Stock A will grow from its current value of $20 per share to a value between $24 and $30, you are less optimistic for the prospects for Stock A. You think that the final value after one year's time will be somewhere between $18 and $24 per share. Also, assume that a one-year stock put option contract is available with a strike price of $24, and that the price of this contract is $2. As with all stock options in this book, if you decide to place your $2 bet by purchasing a stock put option contract, you must wait the full year in order to see if your bet actually pays off.

If you really, really, really believe that Stock A is going to drop in value to $18, then the stock put option contract might be a good investment. Instead of just holding on to your $20, you could buy 10 stock put options. Then in one year's time, when the stock is trading at a share price of $18, each of your put options will be worth $6. This is the difference between the strike price ($24) and the current market value of Stock A ($18). Since each of your stock put options is worth $6, your total payoff on the ten options will be $60. In short, your $20 investment in the 10 put options has turned into $60 in cash. This again, is a 200% rate of return.

That's the good news. However, if Stock A does not drop in value to $18, but instead rises in value to $24 or more, your stock put option contracts become worthless, and you will have again lost your entire $20 investment. The rate of return possibilities for an investment in the actual stock range from a loss of 10% (the stock drops in value from $20 to $18) to a gain of 20% (the stock increases in value from $20 to $24). However, the rate of return range on an investment in stock put option was much wider. The stock put option returns ranged from a 100% loss to a 200% gain, based on the same market behavior that produced a -10% to 20% range of rates of return on the actual stock. Investing in stock put option contracts is much riskier than investing in the stock itself.

THE FULL RANGE OF STOCK OPTION INVESTMENTS

Both of the above illustrations, one involving a stock call option contract and one involving a stock put option contract, highlight a key fact of option investments. It is possible to make money in options no matter what the market does. Whether the market price of Stock A went up or the market price of Stock A went down, it was possible to find an option contract that returned a gain. Every horse race has a winner. But keep in mind that it was also possible to find an option contract which returned a loss. There are always lots of losing horses in any horse race. Investing in option contracts, or playing the ponies at the local race track, is definitely not for those who fear risk or who are afraid of losing their entire investment in the case of options or bet in the case of horse racing.

To make matters even more complex, an investor has the choice of either buying a stock put option contract or a stock call option contract, or has the choice of selling either contract. In other words, instead of spending the $2 to buy one of the contracts, the investor could decide to take someone else's $2 bet. But in this case, the investor takes on the responsibility for paying off on the contract at the end of the contract's term.

Consider the two sample options that were shown above, and the various investment choices, depending upon what an investor thinks the stock may do in the future. The two option contracts are:

Stock A Call Option Contract: The term is one year and the strike price is $24 per share. The contract is selling for $2.

Stock A Put Option Contract: The term is one year and the strike price is $24 per share. The contract is selling for $2.

If you really believe that Stock A will rise to $30 per share, then a good bet would be to buy the stock call option contract. You will turn your $2 bet into a $6 gain – a 200% return. If you really believe that Stock A will drop to $18 per share, then a good bet would be to buy the stock put option contract. You will again turn your $2 bet into a $6 gain – a 200% return.

However, if you believe that Stock A will only rise to a value of about $24, the strike price of either contract, then perhaps your better bet will not be to purchase either contract, but to sell them. In this case you get the $2, which is paid to you by the person buying a contract. If the actual price of Stock A turns out to be $24, you get to keep the $2. But if the actual price of Stock A turns out to be anything other than $24, you will be responsible for making the payoff. As noted above, the payoffs could become expensive. If you are required to pay out more than the $2 you received for selling the option contract, you will lose money on your decision to sell a contract rather than to buy one.

Stock options are a very diverse set of investments. Given that an investor may either buy or sell a given contract, it is always possible to find a contract that will definitely pay something in the future. It is also always possible to find a contract that will definitely generate a loss in the future. Stock options are a very risky investment alternative.

STOCK OPTION PRICING

In each of the above illustrations, the stock option contract price was shown as $2. This number was selected to help emphasize that a $2 option contract is not a whole lot different from a $2 bet at the local horse racing track. But stock options are different from horse racing bets. At the horse races, you decide how much you want to bet, and then the payoff varies depending upon how many other people decide to bet on the same horse. This leads to a natural question: How (or who) determines the price of a stock option contract?

The answer is that stock option contract prices are determined by the market in the same way that basic stock prices are determined. Stock options are publicly traded, and the option price reflects the price that a willing buyer and a willing seller agree upon as the price for the option. For a stock call option contract, there is buyer of the contract, who hopes that the underlying share will grow to a value in excess of the strike price, and there is a seller (or writer) of the contract, who hopes that the stock price stays below the strike price. For a stock put option contract, there is a buyer of the contract, who hopes that the underlying share will drop to a value below the strike price, and there is a seller (or writer) of the contract, who hopes that the stock price stays above the strike price. In either case the willing buyer and willing seller strike a bargain as to what they believe the appropriate price of the "bet" on the future value of a share of stock should be.

As shown above, the ultimate value of a given stock option contract rests on what happens to the share price of the underlying stock over the term of the contract. If you purchase a stock call option, and the price of the underlying share grows to a value that is well beyond the strike price, you will be happy with your purchase. If you purchase a stock put option, and the stock price drops to a value that is well below the strike price, again you will be happy with your purchase. If you make your purchases in the opposite direction, i.e., you purchase a call option and the share value falls to a level below the strike price, or you purchase a put option and the share value grows to a price larger than the strike price, you will receive nothing for your investment. You will have incurred a 100% loss.

Given that the value for an option contract is so intimately tied to what happens to the price of the underlying stock, it seems natural to develop some sort of formula that relates the price of the option contract to anticipated behavior of the underlying security. Having such a formula would be a huge help to an investor who is considering a stock option purchase.

THE BLACK-SCHOLES STOCK OPTION PRICING MODEL

The best known formula that is designed to relate the price of a stock call option contract to the expected behavior of the underlying security is the Black-Scholes Stock Option Pricing Model. This formula was published in 1973 by Fischer Black and Myron Scholes, and has been considered to be a huge breakthrough in the field of stock option pricing. The very basic model uses five key factors to estimate the price of a stock call option: the current selling price of the underlying stock, the strike price, the term of the option contract, the risk-free rate of return, and the anticipated volatility of the underlying stock. For the curious, the Black-Scholes model is described in more detail in Appendix 3.

There is a related formula to describe the estimated value of a stock put option. One of the amazing features of either the stock call option formula or the stock put option formula is that it does not reference the expected rate of return on the underlying security as a relevant variable in option pricing. This point is almost universally described in finance textbooks as being surprising. Given that the payoff on an option contract depends completely upon the future value of the underlying share of stock, to not have the expected return be a relevant variable does seem to be a bit unusual.

One critical assumption, which is part of the Black-Scholes Stock Option Pricing Model, is that future stock prices may be modeled using the lognormal probability density function. The specific lognormal probability density function for the model is the same one that was shown to be quite inaccurate in the busting of Myth 3. Also, the Black-Scholes model uses an arithmetic mean of historical returns as part of the process for determining a key parameter describing the volatility of the underlying stock. If the underlying stock has wide swings in value, this parameter is large; if the underlying stock has had a history of stable values, this parameter is small. But as shown in the busting of Myth 1, there is no unique arithmetic mean that can be derived from historical data.

In both of these critical areas, the Black-Scholes model is treating historical investment returns as if they were independently determined events, not conditional events. Based on the first three busted myths, this would seem to present accuracy problems for the Black-Scholes Stock Option Pricing Model. These accuracy problems, meaning that the Black-Scholes estimates for the value of an option contract are deviating from the actual market quotations, have in fact surfaced and most leading academics are now well aware of them.

CURRENT STATUS OF THE BLACK-SCHOLES STOCK OPTION PRICING MODEL

Given the dependence of the Black-Scholes model on the myths that were busted in Chapters 3, 4, and 5, it would seem to be a natural consequence that the Black-Scholes model would be having some serious accuracy problems. This is, in fact, the case. To confirm these problems one needs only to turn to some of the modern finance technical articles.

For example, Mark Rubinstein in a 1994 Presidential Address to the American Finance Association noted that: "… Black-Scholes has become increasingly unreliable over time in the very markets where one would expect it to be most accurate …"; Torben Andersen in his 2002 paper: *An Empirical Investigation of Continuous Time Equity Return Models* wrote: "… Black-Scholes … is well known to produce pronounced and persistent biases …"; and David S. Bates documented many problems with the Black-Scholes model in his 2002 paper, *Empirical Option Pricing: A Retrospection.*

In one candid exchange with a leading member of the academic finance community, I learned that: "There is not only a 'concern' about accuracy [of the Black-Scholes formula]; that formula is way off market prices, especially for well out of the money or long dated options. Academics have essentially abandoned the Black-Scholes model for serious option pricing applications."

While I appreciate the candor of this particular professor, I am left with the uncomfortable feeling that the business community, which has relied heavily on the Black-Scholes model for expensing employee stock options, is not as aware of the Black-Scholes problems as the academic community.

THE STOCK OPTION MYTH BUSTING ILLUSTRATIONS

The next three chapters will be used to bust three very important myths in stock option pricing. In doing so, the illustrations will also describe the reasons that the Black-Scholes model is experiencing the accuracy problems mentioned above. In keeping with the spirit of this book, the myths presented in the next three chapters will all be busted using actual data illustrations. Although the myths will be busted using actual data, there is a mathematical basis that drives the myth-busting process. Hence, the issue under consideration is much broader than the particular data set used for the illustration, and the point being made, since it is mathematical in nature, could be illustrated with many other sets of data.

The data used for these illustrations will be the same Ibbotson large company data that has been used all along. In order to create a call or put option for illustration purposes, the Ibbotson large company stock Index will be used. For example, as of January 1, 2008, this index was at $3,246. This number could be considered to be the current selling price of a security, which in turn makes it possible to consider both call and put options on the Ibbotson large company stock index.

Continuing the example, a 3-year stock call option with a strike price of $4,000 is a contract that would allow a person to make a bet on the anticipated value of the Ibbotson large company stock index on January 1, 2011. This contract (bet) would be worth nothing on January 1, 2011, if the Ibbotson

Index is less than $4,000. However, if the index is greater than $4,000, the stock call option contract will have value. For example, if the index on that date were $5,000, then the stock call option would be worth $1,000 at that time, as this is the difference between the actual index ($5,000) and the strike price ($4,000) on January 1, 2011.

The role of an option pricing model is to place a current price (as of January 1, 2008) on the stock call option contract. How much would a willing buyer and a willing seller agree upon as the appropriate "bet" to make on January 1, 2008, concerning the Ibbotson large company stock index at a fixed price of $4,000 on January 1, 2011?

Finally, and as noted before, in these illustrations the holder of the option will only be able to take advantage of the option's provisions on the last day of the term of the option contract. In other words, it is assumed that the stock option's value will only be determined at the last day of the term of the contract. This is the same basic assumption that underlies the Black-Scholes model as well.

With that as background, let's press on with some more myth busting!

Peter Ponders a Profitable Plan

Chapter 7

MYTH 4: HEDGED EQUITY TRADING AGAINST A SINGLE OPTION CONTRACT PROVIDES AN ARBITRAGE OPPORTUNITY

Our friend Pete knew just what to do,

when spotting a seller and buyer, too.

For a mere ten bucks, he'd buy what he'd seen;

but then right away, he would take in fifteen.

Visions of riches came into clear view.

Our friend Pete knew just what to do.

MYTH 4: HEDGED EQUITY TRADING AGAINST A SINGLE OPTION CONTRACT PROVIDES AN ARBITRAGE OPPORTUNITY

As with some previous myths, Myth 4 has some very technical language. The challenge will be to illustrate exactly what Myth 4 is saying, and why Myth 4 is not true. Since the assumption that Myth 4 is true drives the entire Black-Scholes theory of option pricing, the busting of this one myth will have a significant impact in the field of option pricing estimates. This will affect investors who want to actually trade in listed stock option contracts and will affect companies that have been using the Black-Scholes formula to disclose the value of employee stock options as a corporate expense item.

ARBITRAGE

Before examining the role that arbitrage might play in stock option pricing, it is necessary to gain a feel for what arbitrage is and how the arbitrage potential affects all market prices. An arbitrage opportunity occurs when there is a mismatch in a given market, and this mismatch allows an individual to make a guaranteed return without risk. The person who spots the arbitrage opportunity is handed a golden opportunity to make "free money." There may be some small administrative action the person needs to take, but the complete lack of risk is essential for any course of action to be truly labeled as an arbitrage opportunity.

To illustrate a classic arbitrage opportunity, consider what happened to Dave and Deana from Denver last Tuesday. They were walking down Lincoln Street when they noticed a street vendor selling miniature Denver Bronco footballs for $10 each. After they turned the corner onto Colfax Avenue they noticed that a Denver Bronco fan had set up a card table and was offering to purchase the identical miniature Denver Bronco footballs for $15 each. Dave and Deana looked at each other and decided to take advantage of the quick easy gain arbitrage opportunity. While Deana chatted with the fan, Dave walked back to the vendor and bought a miniature football for $10. He then returned to the fan to sell the football for $15, pocketing the $5 gain. Then Deana repeated the same exercise, remembering the advice on the shampoo bottle: lather, rinse, but most importantly, repeat.

Presumably Dave and Deana could repeat the process until such time as the buyer and seller of the miniature footballs realized what was happening and the seller would raise his price, and/or the buyer would lower his until the arbitrage potential disappears. In other words the potential for an arbitrage opportunity forces a change in the original pricing of miniature Denver Bronco footballs in this very limited market.

A true arbitrage opportunity affects the dynamics of the market. The market simply will not allow an arbitrage opportunity to exist for long. Markets are too transparent, and an easy gain such as the one illustrated above is just too tempting a target. Before long the vendor and the buyer of miniature footballs would be inundated with "customers." The miniature football business dynamic at the corner of Lincoln Street and Colfax Avenue would change.

HEDGED EQUITY TRADING AGAINST A SINGLE OPTION CONTRACT

But just as adept as Dave and Deana are at spotting an arbitrage opportunity, they are equally adept at spotting a situation which may look like an arbitrage possibility but really is not.

Why just last month their neighbor, Carl Cantmiss, tried to talk them into an investment that he said was an arbitrage opportunity. He assured them that the return was "guaranteed" and that there was no possible reason that Dave and Deana would not want to take advantage of this golden opportunity. Dave and Deana were suspicious, but they were also curious to learn more about this "free money" opportunity that Carl had stumbled across.

Carl Cantmiss had found a stock call option contract that appeared to him to be mispriced. The stock call option was a one-year option for Stock A, which had a strike price of $125. The stock call option was selling for $30, and according to Carl's calculations it should have been selling for something less. Carl was sure that he had identified a significant opportunity to make a no-risk arbitrage gain, and he wanted to share his find with Dave and Deana.

Based on the fact that Stock A was currently selling for $100 per share, Carl had figured out a way to make a guaranteed return no matter what happened to Stock A over the course of the year. Carl's plan was as follows:

(1) He would write (sell) two of the stock call option contracts. The purchasers of the contracts would each pay Carl $30, for a total of $60 in cash.

(2) He would borrow an additional $40 from the bank at 8% interest. By taking the loan Carl knew he would be obligated to pay back $43.20 at the end of the year. This $43.20 loan repayment will consist of $40 principle and $3.20 interest.

(3) He would then use the $100 ($60 from writing the options plus $40 that was borrowed) to buy one share of stock.

Now Carl was getting really excited. His arms were waving and he had a grin from ear to ear. He was about to explain that no matter what happened to Stock A, he was sure to make

$6.80, with absolutely no risk. He first explained to Dave and Deana what would happen if Stock A dropped in value. He illustrated his point by assuming that Stock A decreases in value from $100 to $50. Carl said that in this case he owes nothing on the two stock call option contracts that he wrote, since the share price would be less than the strike price of $125. Furthermore, he could sell the share of stock that he bought for its then current value of $50. This will allow him to repay the loan ($43.20) and make a gain of $6.80 with no cash outlay. Free money!!!

To illustrate what might happen if Stock A increases in value; Carl assumed that Stock A might grow from $100 to $200. Carl knew that in this case he would need to make good on the two stock call options with strike prices of $125 that he wrote. Thus, he would owe the difference between the then current stock price of $200 and the strike price of $125 for each option. This obligation would be $75 for each option or $150 in total. But the absolute beauty of Carl's plan is that he would only need to sell the one share of stock that he bought at its then current value of $200. He would first use the proceeds to pay the $150 he owes on the two stock call options. This still leaves him with $50 in cash which he would use to repay the loan ($43.20), leaving him again with a gain of $6.80. Free money!!! No matter what happens to Stock A, Carl is sure that he will make $6.80. Free money has just fallen into his lap.

THE PROBLEM WITH THE ILLUSTRATION AND THE LACK OF AN ARBITRAGE OPPORTUNITY

Dave and Deana listened to Carl's pitch, but then they spotted a very serious problem with the Carl's analysis. The problem with Carl's anticipated windfall is that it depends completely upon Carl's assumptions about future market behavior. In the above simple example, Carl assumed that the only possible future values for the $100 share of stock were a gain to $200 or a loss to $50. This assumption is very critical. It is this assumption which enables Carl Cantmiss to identify the supposedly mispriced $30 option and to do the calculations which supported his claim that there would be a no-risk $6.80 gain.

Dave asked Carl to consider what happens if Stock A actually rises to $300, not $200. Carl, who formerly thought he was guaranteed a free $6.80, now realized that he would be faced with the prospect of paying off $175 on each of the two options (the difference between the share price of $300 and the strike price of $125), plus a loan repayment of $43.20 for a total liability of $175 + $175 + $43.20 = $393.20. His only asset would be the one share of stock worth $300. Suddenly his $6.80 "guaranteed" return has turned into a $93.20 loss. Oops!

Deana then asked Carl to consider what happens if Stock A actually drops in value to $30 instead of $50. Carl then realized that he would have also been disappointed. In this situation Carl does not owe anything on the two stock call options that he would write, but he would still owe $43.20 to the bank. His only asset would be the share of stock that is worth $30. He loses $13.20 on his loan repayment. Double oops!

Clearly the arbitrage potential that Carl had thought would provide him with a guaranteed return turns out to be quite illusory. As pointed out in the miniature football example, if a situation is to be described as an arbitrage opportunity, there truly has to be no down-side risk. Real arbitrage opportunities require no (repeat, NO) assumptions. In real arbitrage situations, the clever investor who spots the golden opportunity just needs to follow a certain course of action, and free money will flow into his pocket.

In Carl's situation, he had made an assumption about the future volatility of Stock A. His assumption was that the volatility could be described by the $200/$50 scenario. However, as Dave and Deana pointed out, if the actual volatility is something different than what Carl had assumed, Carl's guaranteed return could turn into a big loss very quickly.

Carl's proposed plan of action is known as hedged equity trading against a single option contract. This investment scheme requires a volatility assumption, and getting the wrong assumption can cause big (repeat, BIG) problems. Carl began to have big doubts about what he formerly thought was a golden opportunity.

ALTERNATIVE HEDGING STRATEGIES

In his illustration of a hedged equity trading arbitrage gain, Carl assumed that the volatility characteristics of Stock A could be described by the scenario where the only two choices for stock movement were an increase to $200 per share or a decrease to $50 per share. By making this particular assumption, Carl thought that the appropriate option price was $26.85. Given Carl's assumptions, this is the only price where it is not possible to create some hedged position that returns a gain. However, Carl would still need to choose between two exactly opposite hedging strategies.

Continuing the illustration using the $200/$50 assumption, if the actual option price is more than this $26.85 number, such as the $30 stock call option that Carl had spotted, the following hedged position will always return a gain:

(1) Write two option contracts.

(2) Borrow the additional amount necessary to buy one share of stock.

(3) Use these two sources of money to actually buy the one share of stock.

But if Carl had made a different volatility assumption, such as one where the only two choices for stock movement were an increase to $300 per share or a decrease to $30 per share, the estimated appropriate option price changes. Under this particular assumption the only option price where it is not possible to create some hedged position that returns a gain is an option price of $46.81. Under this assumption the $30 option that Carl had spotted was actually underpriced, not overpriced. In situations where the option is underpriced, it is the exact opposite of the above hedging strategy, which will always return a gain:

(1) Sell one share of the stock short. This is a transaction where buyer gives you the current price of the stock, and in return, you promise to provide the buyer with a share of stock at a fixed later date.

(2) Use the proceeds from the short sale to buy two stock call option contracts.

(3) Invest any leftover funds at the bank.

In modern finance textbooks the above types of illustration are often used to show how the market would force the mispriced $30 option down to its necessary price of $26.85 or up to its necessary price of $46.81. The market simply would not let a multitude of clever investors make "free money." But in all these illustrations, it is assumed that the clever investor "knows" enough about future market behavior to correctly adopt the right hedging strategy. Any time future market behavior is assumed to be known, watch out!

Future market behavior is never known, and making the assumption that it is can be a mistake, a very big mistake.

If future volatility is described by the $200/$50 scenario, then $26.85 seems like it might be the right option price. But if future volatility is described by the more volatile $300/$30 scenario, then $46.81 seems like it might be the right option price. Given that no one (repeat, NO ONE) knows for certain what future volatility will be, it becomes impossible to tell whether the $30 option is either overpriced or underpriced. It becomes impossible to select the right hedging strategy with 100% certainty.

ONE STRATEGY ALWAYS PAYS; ONE STRATEGY ALWAYS LOSES

Carl Cantmiss, by assuming the $200/$50 scenario, thought the $30 option was overpriced. But perhaps he should have assumed the $300/$30 scenario in which case the $30 option would be underpriced. If the first assumption is incorrect, it will lead Carl into adopting the wrong hedging strategy, thus locking in his losses instead of his gains.

Based on his assumptions, Carl thought he was guaranteed a $6.80 return no matter what happened to the future value of the stock. In the illustration shown above Carl took three actions:

(1) He wrote two stock call option contracts, bringing in a total of $60.

(2) He borrowed $40 from the bank at 8.0% interest, obligating a payback of $43.20.

(3) He bought one share of stock for $100.

When the share price rises to $300 instead of the assumed value of $200, this three-step strategy turns out to produce a $93.20 loss, not the $6.80 supposedly "guaranteed" gain.

But if Carl had only switched strategies, his $93.20 loss would have become a $93.20 gain. He should have adopted the strategy that is appropriate if the option appears to be underpriced. In this case, Carl should have:

(1) Sold one share of stock short to bring in a total of $100. This is a transaction where Carl accepts the current price of a share of stock in exchange for a promise to provide a share of stock at a fixed later date.

(2) Used $60 of this amount to buy two $30 stock call options.

(3) Invest the remaining $40 at 8.0% interest for an ending balance of $43.20

In other words instead of writing the two option contracts, borrowing at the risk-free rate, and buying a share of stock, he should have taken the exact opposite actions. He should have sold a share of the security short, taken the proceeds to buy two stock call option contracts, and then invested the balance at the risk-free rate. This is the strategy for a stock call option that is underpriced, and will produce a gain no matter whether the security rises to $300 in value or sinks to $30 in value.

If the security rises to $300 per share, Carl makes $175 on each of the two options that he bought producing a $350 gain. He uses $300 of this amount to make good on the share of stock he sold short. The remaining $50 is added to the $43.20 in the bank to make a gain of $93.20. If the security sinks to $30 per share, the two stock call options Carl bought are worth nothing, but he can take the $43.20 from the bank, use $30 to make good on the share he sold short, and keep the remaining $13.20.

Since the two strategies shown above are exact opposites, one strategy will always produce a gain, and the other will always produce a loss. If a clever investor hopes to make a gain, he needs to make an assumption as to which strategy is the right one. Adopting the wrong strategy only locks in the not-so-clever investor's losses.

THE BLACK-SCHOLES THEORY

Modern mathematical presentations of the Black-Scholes stock option pricing formula go to great lengths using sophisticated mathematical techniques such as stochastic calculus, Ito's Lemma, and Girsanov's Theorem to demonstrate that the Black-Scholes value for an option is the unique value for an option contract that will not allow the creation of some hedged position to return a gain to an investor. But there is a different Black-Scholes value for the option contract for each different volatility assumption. This is not unlike the elementary illustrations shown above where the unique value of $26.85 was appropriate if the volatility is described by the $200/$50 scenario, but $46.81 is the unique value if volatility is described by the $300/$30 scenario. In the simple illustrations shown above these truly are the unique values for which it is not possible to find a hedged equity trading strategy that will produce a positive return, given the particular volatility assumption.

However, to conclude that this unique Black-Scholes value is the option price requires an additional argument. This second argument assumes that a clever investor knows future volatility with sufficient accuracy to be able to always pick the right hedging strategy and would thus be able to force any mispriced option either up or down to its Black-Scholes value. The clever investor is able to identify future volatility with such accuracy that the hedging strategies described above have the power to move the actual option prices to their unique Black-Scholes values. This ability to move markets is just like the arbitrage opportunity in miniature footballs that was able to change the original pricing structure in that limited market. But picking the right hedging strategy turns out to be pretty darn hard.

If the actual price of the option exceeds the Black-Scholes value, as was the case in the simple \$200/\$50 illustration above, the hedging strategy consists of writing option contracts, borrowing from the bank, and buying shares of the underlying security. If the actual price of the option is below the Black-Scholes value, as was the case in the simple \$300/\$30 illustration above, another strategy is appropriate. This alternative strategy requires the exact opposite actions and involves selling the underlying security short, buying the option contracts, and investing the difference in the bank.

For any clever investor to realize his gain from a mispriced option, the clever investor must actually decide which of these two strategies is the correct one, create the right hedged position, and change it continually, assuming that there are no transaction costs. Clearly, this type of "arbitrage" is significantly different from other forms of true arbitrage that affect the prices of stock options, such as an arbitrage opportunity known as put-call parity. For the curious, illustrations of true arbitrage opportunities in stock options where there is no risk no matter what the market does are provided in Appendix 4.

All of these points lead to the question: Is hedged equity trading really an arbitrage opportunity? The practical realities associated with the hedged equity approach are too significant to overcome. It is mathematically impossible to provide a guaranteed hedged equity arbitrage return using only a single option contract. This is because the investment process needed to realize such a gain requires the investor to decide whether the particular option is either overpriced or underpriced, and apply the appropriate hedging strategy. But it is impossible to tell whether any given option was either overpriced or underpriced until the actual market plays out.

If actual market volatility is higher than that which was assumed by the investor seeking the hedged equity arbitrage gain, then the option might turn out to have been underpriced not overpriced. If actual market volatility is less than that which was assumed by the investor seeking the hedged equity arbitrage gain, then again the investor could suffer a loss instead of a gain. Even if perfect assumptions were selected, actual market behavior could deviate from those assumptions for the duration of the option contract, thus producing results that are the exact opposite of what was anticipated. No matter what hedging strategy is adopted by the investor, there is always the possibility of market results that yield a loss.

HEDGED EQUITY TRADING WITH MORE REALISTIC OPTION CONTRACTS

The above illustrations were all quite simplified. Real stock investments have way more than two possible returns. However, the same basic problem shown above exists for all option contracts. For example, consider the following information concerning a stock call option on Stock A:

Current Selling Price of Stock A:	$100
Strike Price in the Option Contract:	$105
Risk-Free Rate of Return:	4%
Option Term:	3 Months
Volatility:	20% to 40%

The volatility shown above has not been specifically identified because the volatility is something that will happen in the future. No matter what historical volatility has been, no one knows for sure what the actual volatility will be for the next three months, which is the term of this particular option contract.

Using the Black-Scholes formula, a stock call option contract would be valued at different prices depending upon the volatility assumption. Table 14 below gives a sampling of what some of these values might be.

Table 14
BLACK-SCHOLES VALUES

Volatility	Stock Call Option Price
40.0%	$6.30
30.0	4.32
20.0	2.39

If there is a traded option on the market that has a current price of $4.32, it is absolutely impossible to tell if future volatility will be 30%, in which case this option appears to be appropriately priced, or if future volatility will be 20% or 40%, in which case the option appears as if it is not priced correctly.

Furthermore, if the future volatility is 20%, the actual contract appears to be overpriced. This means the hedging strategy to try to make an "arbitrage" gain involves writing some options, borrowing from the bank, and buying the underlying security. If the future volatility is 40%, the actual contract appears to be underpriced. This means that the strategy to try to make an "arbitrage" gain involves buying some options, selling the underlying security short, and investing with the bank. These strategies are exact opposites. If one will produce a gain, the other will produce a loss. Yet it is impossible to tell which strategy is the right one to implement.

Some members of the modern finance community claim that it is fairly easy to estimate volatility and that the issues described above are not significant. But when one looks at history, volatility can jump around quite a bit. Estimating volatility might not be as easy as some in the modern finance community think that it is. For example, Table 15 below compares two different two-week periods worth of activity in the S&P 500 Stock Index.

Table 15
S&P 500 STOCK INDEX
VOLATILITY COMPARISON

August 11 - 22, 2008				November 3 - 14, 2008			
Date	Previous Close	Change	Percent	Date	Previous Close	Change	Percent
8/11	$1,206.32	$9.00	0.69	11/3	$968.77	$2.47	0.25
8/12	1,305.32	16.13	1.24	11/4	966.30	39.45	4.08
8/13	1,289.19	3.36	0.26	11/5	1,005.75	52.98	5.27
8/14	1,285.83	7.10	0.55	11/6	952.77	47.89	5.03
8/15	1,292.93	5.27	0.41	11/7	904.88	26.11	2.89
8/18	1,298.20	19.60	1.51	11/10	930.99	11.78	1.27
8/19	1,278.60	11.91	0.93	11/11	919.21	20.26	2.20
8/20	1,266.69	7.85	0.62	11/12	898.95	46.60	5.18
8/21	1,274.54	3.18	0.25	11/13	852.30	58.99	6.92
8/22	1,277.72	14.48	1.13	11/14	911.29	38.00	4.17
Average Daily Percent Change: 0.76%				Average Daily Percent Change: 3.73%			

The above table shows that for two different two-week periods that were only three months apart, the average daily percentage change (either positive or negative) in the S&P 500 Stock Index varied from 0.76% to 3.73%. The second number is nearly five times the first. Perhaps it is not as easy to estimate future volatility as modern finance would like investors to believe.

This issue is significant, since if hedged equity trading is not arbitrage, the basic argument that underpins the Black-Scholes theory is lost. This allows other market forces, such as the expected rate of return on the underlying security, to come into play in estimating reasonable prices of option contracts. These new market forces would reflect the factors that would encourage willing buyers and writers to actually enter into the transaction. The new estimated option prices would be different from their unique Black-Scholes values.

DRAMATIC DEMONSTRATION: LONG-TERM CAPITAL MANAGEMENT

So far this chapter has shown the difficulties with hedged equity trading and how it involves significant risk. Other stock option arbitrage opportunities such as put-call parity are true risk-free arbitrage opportunities. A clever investor can identify a put-call parity situation and realize a gain. Put-call parity requires no assumptions about future market behavior. Put-call parity has the ability to move option prices.

In contrast, hedged equity trading against a single option contract requires an assumption about future volatility, and if this assumption is not made correctly, hedged equity trading against a single option contract can generate significant losses. This situation leads to the most dramatic of the dramatic demonstrations in this book.

The ideas presented in this chapter were actually demonstrated in practice. The firm of Long-Term Capital Management was founded in 1993 based on the concept that it could identify mispriced options and by engaging in hedged equity trading, return a substantial profit to its investors. The firm began with a very promising start, but then the firm imploded after only a four-year existence. The collapse jeopardized not just the big Wall Street banks that it relied on for financing, but the entire financial system. The story of Long-Term Capital

Management's rise and fall is detailed in Roger Lowenstein's best selling book, *When Genius Failed*.

At the time of Long-Term Capital Management's failure, leading academics attributed the failure to not using a long enough history for selecting a volatility assumption. The much more important point, however, is that no history can guarantee a hedged equity trading return. Simply put, hedged equity trading against a single option contract is not an arbitrage opportunity.

Max Solves His Problem of Losing Variables

Chapter 8

MYTH 5: THE EXPECTED RATE OF RETURN ON THE UNDERLYING SECURITY IS NOT A RELEVANT VARIABLE IN OPTION PRICING

Math man Max loves his work; that is clear.

But darned if an "X" doesn't just disappear.

That yields an answer that's really quite funny.

An unusual fix turns his sad mood to sunny.

MYTH 5: THE EXPECTED RATE OF RETURN ON THE UNDERLYING SECURITY IS NOT A RELEVANT VARIABLE IN OPTION PRICING

Certainly the most surprising conclusion reached by Dr. Black and Dr. Scholes when they published their landmark 1973 paper on option pricing is that the expected rate of return on the underlying security was not a relevant variable in option pricing. This result runs counter to common logic – after all the basic option contract only pays off based on what happens to the underlying security! This raises a great question: If common sense seems to say that this variable should be important in option pricing, what happened to it in the development of the Black-Scholes formula?

The surprising answer is that during the course of the development of the Black-Scholes formula, the risk-free rate of return gets substituted for a more realistic expected rate of return on the underlying security. The Black-Scholes formula determines option prices under the assumption that the expected rate of return on the underlying security is the risk-free rate of return. The expected rate of return on the underlying security is important, it is just that the Black-Scholes formula, by relying on the assumption that Myth 4 is true, sets this variable at the risk-free rate.

This statement is so important, it bears repeating one more time. The Black-Scholes formula determines option prices under the assumption that the expected rate of return on the underlying security is the risk-free rate of return. The stock option estimates for Microsoft stock assume that Microsoft stock has an expected rate of return equal to the risk-free rate of return. The stock option estimates for General Motors stock assume that the General Motors stock has an expected rate of return equal to the risk-free rate of return. The stock option estimates for the S&P 500 Index assume that the S&P 500 Index has an expected rate of return equal to the risk-free rate of return. Given that investors in options are likely to assume an expected rate of return for the underlying security that is different from the risk-free rate, this critical "assumption" in the Black-Scholes model likely accounts for many of the model's well-documented accuracy issues.

The substitution of the risk-free rate for a more realistic expected rate of return on the underlying security can be demonstrated mathematically, and it is possible to pinpoint exactly where in the original 1973 Black and Scholes paper that the substitution occurs. But this book is about demonstrations, not mathematics, and the detailed illustrations presented in this chapter are designed to confirm this point for all audiences with the use of actual data. For the curious, the mathematical demonstration is presented in Appendix 5.

TEN-YEAR OPTION ILLUSTRATIONS

Let's catch up with our friends Dave and Deana from Denver one more time. On January 1, 2008, Dave and Deana made a New Year's resolution to consider stock options as part of their expanded investment portfolio. True to their nature, Dave and Deana decided to do some independent research before actually making any investment. They began their study of this important topic by considering what might happen if they make an investment in ten-year put or ten-year call options on the Ibbotson Large Company Stock Index. As of January 1, 2008, this index was $3,246. If they picked a strike price of $4,579 and used reasonable assumptions in the well-known Black-Scholes stock option pricing formula, the estimated price for either the stock put option or the stock call option is about $680.

Dave and Deana both realized that they would be making a "bet" on the value of the Ibbotson Large Company Stock Index. But being horse racing fans, they were fairly comfortable analyzing possible bets. They knew that there would be risks, but they realized that there might be the potential for great rewards.

In the case of the put option bet, they would have paid $680 on January 1, 2008, and will only get any money back if the Ibbotson Large Company Stock Index is less than $4,579 on January 1, 2018. In the case of the call option bet, they would have paid $680 on January 1, 2008, and will only get back any money if the Ibbotson Large Company Stock Index is more than $4,579 on January 1, 2018. In either case, the amount of money that gets paid back would be the difference between the Ibbotson Index on January 1, 2018, and the strike price of $4,579.

Dave and Deana talked about this $680 price for either option, and something just didn't seem quite right. Based on their understanding of general stock market expectations the put option price seems way too high and the call option price seems way too low. They decided to use the *SBBI Yearbook* large company stock return data to make a "reasonableness check" of the two $680 option prices. They used the actual historical data to see what might happen with their proposed investment if these historical returns should happen again in the future.

For example, if over the ten years 2008-2017, the Ibbotson Large Company Stock Index mirrors what happened in 1965-1974, then the stock put option contract described above will provide a positive payoff. Large company stock performance over the period 1965-1974 averaged 1.2% per year. Applying this percentage to the January 1, 2008 Index of $3,246 for 10 years yields an estimated Index of $3,672 on January 1, 2018. Their $680 investment in the stock put option contract will generate a payoff of $907, as this is the difference between the strike price of $4,579 and the estimated Index of $3,672.

On the other hand, if over the ten years 2008-2017 the Ibbotson Large Company Stock Index mirrors what happened in 1951-1960, the stock call option contract described above will provide a positive payoff. Large company stock performance over the period 1951-1960 averaged 16.2% per year. Applying this percentage to the January 1, 2008, Index of $3,246 for 10 years yields an estimated Index of $14,570 on January 1, 2018. Their $680 investment in the stock call option contract will generate a payoff of $9,991, as this is the difference between the estimated Index of $14,570 and the strike price of $4,579.

Starting with the ten-year period 1926-1935 and ending with the period 1998-2007, the *SBBI Yearbook* has data for 73 different time periods of 10 consecutive calendar years. Dave took on the challenge of repeating the exercise of estimating the potential payoff from the $680 put option contract described above for all 73 historical ten-year periods. When doing this research he found out that the put option contract would have generated a positive payoff for only seven out of the 73 historical periods.

For the other 66 historical ten-year periods the estimated January 1, 2018, Ibbotson Index would exceed the strike price of $4,579. This means that the put option contract would be worthless, and Dave and Deana would have spent $680 for nothing. Table 16 below shows the complete details of Dave's research:

Table 16

ESTIMATED PAYOFF ON PUT OPTION CONTRACT WITH STRIKE PRICE OF $4,579 IF 2008-2017 RETURN MATCHES RETURN FOR INDICATED TEN-YEAR PERIOD

Historical Period	Average Annual Return	Estimated Index on January 1, 2018	Estimated Payoff on Put Option Contract
1928-1937	0.0%	$3,252.00	$1,327.00
1929-1938	-0.9	2,969.00	1,610.00
1930-1939	0.0	3,229.00	1,350.00
1931-1940	1.8	3,879.00	700.00
1965-1974	1.2	3,672.00	907.00
1966-1975	3.3	4,480.00	99.00
1969-1978	3.2	4,431.00	148.00
All Other Periods	More Than 3.5%	More than $4,579	0.00
Total Payoff for all 73 Periods			$6,141.00
Average Payoff per Period for all 73 Periods			$84.00

Using the Black-Scholes formula, Dave realized that he was being asked to pay $680 for a contract that would have averaged only an $84 payoff over the last 73 historical ten-year periods. Dave did not see paying $680 for an option contract that has had an average historical payoff of only $84 when looking at the last 73 ten-year periods as being a particularly good investment alternative! While history is no guarantee of what may happen in the future, the degree of difference, and the length of the history, gave Dave lots of reason to be very concerned. He began to wonder how in the world the Black-Scholes formula came up with the price of $680 for an investment that appears to be worth much, much less.

Deana took on the challenge of repeating the exercise for all 73 historical ten-year periods for the $680 call option contract. She learned that the call option contract would have generated a positive payoff for 66 of the periods, and the average payoff for all 73 periods would have been $5,733. Using the Black-Scholes formula, Deana realized that she only had to pay $680 for a contract that has averaged a $5,733 payoff over the last 73 historical ten-year periods.

She thought that this seemed like it might be a pretty darn good investment alternative! If she were to do that well over the period 2008-2017, her $680 investment will have had an annual rate of return of 24%. Again, while there is no guarantee that history will repeat itself, the degree of difference between the $680 price of the option contract and the estimated $5,733 average payoff caused Deana to also be concerned. She, too, began to wonder how in the world the Black-Scholes formula came up with the price of $680 for an investment which appears to be worth much, much more.

Dave and Deana then shared their findings with each other. This raised their interest even farther into finding out how the Black-Scholes formula produced the two $680 option prices. They were aware that the formula is very famous, but they did not want to rely on its fame alone. They wanted to have a better understanding of where the two $680 prices came from. Then Deana came up with an idea for trying to figure out what was happening. This idea involved repeating the same exercise they had just completed, but by using lower rates of return than those that appeared in the *SBBI Yearbook*.

CONFIRMING THAT BLACK-SCHOLES ASSUMES RISK-FREE EXPECTED GROWTH

She wanted to repeat the exercise of using historical results to derive estimated payoffs, but using lower rates of return. She knew that because this new "history" of investment return would have lower values than the actual Ibbotson large company stock return data, Dave's estimated put option payoff would increase, and her estimated call option payoff would decrease.

As a first step in the recalculation process, they reduced every one of the 82 Ibbotson large company annual calendar year returns by 2%. For example, the 28.6% rate for 1998 got reduced to 26.6% and the -11.9% rate for 2001 got reduced to -13.9%. This new modified historical set of rates has the same volatility as the large company stock rates of return shown in the *SBBI Yearbook*, but the arithmetic mean return is reduced by 2%. Since the volatility is the same, the Black-Scholes values for the two ten-year options on this "Ibbotson Large Company Stock Return Data Reduced by 2%" history are still priced at $680 each, using the Black-Scholes formula.

But this new set of data reflects lower rates of return. Dave used this new "history" to recalculate the average historical payoff on the stock put option contract in the illustration. In this case the average payoff is increased from $84 to $168. Deana did the calculations for the average historical payoff on the stock call option contract. In this case the average payoff is reduced from $5,733 to $4,126.

Dave and Deana then repeated this process of lowering actual *SBBI Yearbook* returns by a constant amount until every one of the 82 annual returns was reduced by about 8.7%. Since the volatility is still the same for this "history" as it is for the actual Ibbotson large company stock return data, the Black-

Scholes option prices are still $680 for each option contract. However using this "Ibbotson Large Company Stock Return Data Reduced by 8.7%" history, the average payoff for either the put or call option becomes $960. It was Dave who then figured out that if this number was discounted at the 3.5% risk-free rate for the ten-year duration of either of the two option contracts, the resulting price is $680 for each contract, the Black-Scholes value.

Furthermore, the reduction of 8.7% is the approximate reduction necessary to reduce the actual arithmetic mean return of 12.26% for the 82 calendar years to the risk-free rate of 3.5%. Dave and Deana began to realize that the Black-Scholes formula is calculating option prices under the assumption that the Ibbotson Index will have an expected growth rate of only 3.5%, the risk-free rate. In essence, the formula is determining option prices for a "history" where every single rate of return has been reduced to the point where the arithmetic mean of the history is the risk-free rate of return. The actual price of the option contract is then the expected payoff determined using this reduced history discounted at the risk-free rate of return.

All of this seemed very strange to Dave and Deana. First the actual history gets reduced to the point where the arithmetic mean of the reduced history is the risk-free rate of return. Then this new reduced history is used to determine expected payoffs. These expected payoffs are then discounted under the assumption that the option investor's personal discount rate is also the risk-free rate. It seemed to Dave that options are a very risky investment. The option investor's personal discount rate should theoretically be much larger than the risk-free rate of return.

Given all this lack of comfort, Dave and Deana decided to confirm that this process was also happening in other situations. They repeated the exercise using a 2.0% risk-free rate of return. In this case they needed to reduce each calendar year return by 10.2% in order to match the Black-Scholes values for estimated option prices. When they used a 5.0% risk-free rate of return, they needed to reduce each calendar year Ibbotson return by 7.2%. In each case, they were lowering the actual Ibbotson large company stock return history by a uniform amount to a point where the average return for the new history was just the assumed risk-free rate of return. Then using this history they were able to match the Black-Scholes values, by discounting the expected payoff from the reduced history using the risk-free rate of return.

THREE-MONTH OPTION ILLUSTRATIONS

Dave and Deana started their study of option investments with ten-year option contracts, as it made analyzing the stock option "bet" very easy. Their analysis clearly points out a significant defect in the Black-Scholes methodology. It was easy to confirm that the Black-Scholes prices made for a very poor "bet" when the estimated payoff was determined using the actual stock return history. Only when the actual history was reduced to the point where it had an average return of the risk-free rate did the Black-Scholes prices for the put or call stock option "bet" begin to make sense. But even here the resulting Black-Scholes values had the assumption that the investor's personal discount rate is only the risk-free rate of return. It seems as if, given the risky nature of option investments, that the discount rate should be considerably higher. This topic is also covered in more detail below in the section headed Implicit Assumptions.

While the impact of this problem is dramatically seen by looking at longer-term options, Dave and Deana suspected that the same basic problem affects all option prices, even shorter-term listed options. To confirm this point, they repeated the same basic exercise identified above for option contracts with a three-month term. In this case, the Ibbotson large company stock return data shows quarterly returns for 982 different three-month periods. The first one is January – March 1926; the next one is February – April 1926; and the third one is March – May 1926. The last quarter is October – December 2007.

Dave prepared Table 17 below, which compares the Black-Scholes value for three-month option contracts with the discounted value of the expected option payoff based on the actual historical results. His basic assumptions were as follows:

Selling Price of Ibbotson Index	$3,246
Risk-Free Rate of Return	3.5%
Option Term	3 Months
Volatility	16.8%

Table 17

COMPARISON OF BLACK-SCHOLES VALUES WITH ACTUAL DISCOUNTED HISTORICAL PAYOFFS

Strike Price	Black-Scholes Put Price	Discounted Historical Payoff	Black-Scholes Call Price	Discounted Historical Payoff
$3,200.00	$74.77	$58.30	$148.18	$200.80
3,220.00	83.17	63.78	136.74	186.46
3,240.00	92.14	69.72	125.89	172.56
3,260.00	101.70	76.21	115.61	159.22
3,280.00	111.83	83.42	105.91	146.60
3,300.00	122.53	91.20	96.79	134.57
3,320.00	133.80	99.61	88.23	123.14
3,340.00	145.62	108.65	80.22	112.36

As Dave and Deana had suspected and as was the case with the 10-year options, the Black-Scholes put option prices seem way too large compared with what would have been paid out historically under the terms of a stock put option contract, and the Black-Scholes call option prices seem way too small compared with what would have been paid out historically under the terms of a stock call option contract.

Potential option investors, such as Dave and Deana, may want to be very careful if they are using the Black-Scholes formula as guidance when they are considering the purchase or sale of listed options. As shown by the above table, the Black-Scholes value for an option contract does not mesh well with average historical payoffs. This is particularly a concern for put options, where the average historical payoff at the end of the term of the contract is always smaller than the Black-Scholes "price" which would be paid for the contract.

Out of curiosity, Deana wanted to verify that the Black-Scholes formula is making the "assumption" that the expected rate of return on the underlying security is only going to be the risk-free rate of return. She realized that she could verify this point if she used the monthly data in the *SBBI Yearbook*.

There are 984 months of large company stock return data shown in the *SBBI Yearbook*. The arithmetic mean of these 984 monthly returns is 0.9754%. To develop Table 18 below, Deana reduced every single one of those monthly returns by 0.6883%, so that the new arithmetic mean monthly return is 0.2871%. She made these very specific changes because 0.2871% is exactly the monthly rate of return equivalent to an annual rate of return of 3.5%. Thus, her "discounted historical payoff" shown in the table below reflects a history where the risk-free rate of return of 3.5% has been substituted for the actual rate of return of 12.26%.

Table 18

COMPARISON OF BLACK-SCHOLES VALUES ASSUMING A 3.5% RISK-FREE RATE OF RETURN WITH REDUCED DISCOUNTED HISTORICAL PAYOFFS WHERE THE REDUCED HISTORICAL VALUES REFLECT A 3.5% AVERAGE RATE OF RETURN

Strike Price	Black-Scholes Put Price	Discounted Historical Payoff	Black-Scholes Call Price	Discounted Historical Payoff
$3,200.00	$74.77	$77.59	$148.18	$152.61
3,220.00	83.17	85.00	136.74	140.21
3,240.00	92.14	93.02	125.89	128.40
3,260.00	101.70	101.67	115.61	117.21
3,280.00	111.83	111.02	105.91	106.74
3,300.00	122.53	121.17	96.79	97.01
3,320.00	133.80	131.91	88.23	87.97
3,340.00	145.62	143.32	80.22	79.55

The improved comparison is dramatic. As noted before, it is a mathematically verifiable fact that the Black-Scholes formula substitutes the risk-free rate of return for the expected rate of return on the underlying security when determining Black-Scholes option price estimates. The above table simply illustrates that this is the case.

This same point can also be illustrated as easily using other risk-free rates. In each case once the actual history is reduced by a constant percentage amount so that the new average rate of return is the risk-free rate, this new "history" can be used to replicate the Black-Scholes values. As above, the match between the history-derived values and the Black-Scholes values are not identical. One set of pricing estimates is derived from a formula; the other is derived from raw data. But in all cases the matches are actually quite good.

IMPLICIT ASSUMPTIONS

Some members of the modern finance community are willing to confirm that the Black-Scholes formula does, in fact, assume that the underlying security has an expected rate of return equal to the risk-free rate of return. But they then justify this unusual assumption as being an "implicit assumption," not an explicit one. The explanation of the "implicit assumption" line of reasoning and the problems with it are provided below.

The first step is to gain an understanding of the concept of "implicit assumptions." The concept behind implicit assumptions is that it is possible to make an accurate calculation by using two or more assumptions that are known not to be accurate, but are thought to counterbalance each other. It has sometimes been described as "two wrongs making a right."

To illustrate a situation where implicit assumptions do tend to work, assume that you have a piece of property you are not entitled to convert into cash today, but you will be able to exchange for cash one year from now. Clearly, this piece of property has some value, and although you might not be able to exchange the property directly for cash today, perhaps you might be able to find a willing buyer who would buy your rights to the property.

Such a potential buyer would likely value this investment opportunity by making two assumptions: an assumption about how the value of the actual property will change, and an assumption about his own personal discount rate. For example, the potential buyer might decide that the piece of property could change in value from $1,000 at the start of the year to become $1,120 at the end of the year. This represents a 12% growth in the value of the property. If his personal discount rate is 10%, he might be willing to pay ($1,120)/(1.10)

= \$1,018 for your rights to the property now. At this price he is anticipating getting a 10% return on his \$1,018 investment. Both of these assumptions, the 12% assumed growth rate for the property and the 10% discount rate, are known as "explicit" assumptions. They represent the potential buyer's best estimate of what he thinks actually might happen.

Note that instead of using explicit best estimate assumptions, the potential buyer could have used another pair of assumptions that differed by about 2% to arrive at a similar result. For example, he could have made an admittedly low assumption that the value of the property is expected to grow at a 5% rate. This assumption takes the estimated value of the property itself from \$1,000 to \$1,050. But if this admittedly low assumption is then combined with a personal discount rate, which is also set at an admittedly low rate of 3%, the price that he might be willing to pay becomes (\$1,050)/(1.03) = \$1,019. This new number is about the same as the \$1,018 result he would have obtained using explicit assumptions. These new assumptions, the 5% assumed growth rate and the 3% discount rate, are referred to as implicit assumptions. While neither assumption reflects the potential buyer's best estimate, when they are linked together they will still produce reasonable answers.

The above example is one where implicit assumptions may be used to produce reasonable answers. This does not always happen, and sometimes the use of implicit assumptions will produce answers that are very unreasonable. Stock option pricing is one of those situations.

Returning to stock options, the implicit assumption line of reasoning is that while it is true that the Black-Scholes formula assumes that the expected rate of return on the underlying security is the risk-free rate, this low assumed growth rate is combined with an equally low risk-free discount rate, and that these two admittedly low assumptions counterbalance one another. Even though the original Black and Scholes paper makes no reference to implicit assumptions, those who advocate this line of reasoning maintain that these implicit assumptions justify the Black-Scholes values.

Unfortunately, this line of reasoning has some material problems. Consider an example where the explicit assumptions are that a stock price will grow at 12% rate and that an option investor's personal discount rate is also 12%. The current risk-free rate of return is 4%. Hence, 4% becomes the implicit assumption for the expected rate of return on the underlying security, and 4% also becomes the implicit assumption for the investor's personal discount rate. The estimated option price will be determined by assuming that the stock price will grow at a 4% rate, but the impact of this admittedly low assumption is supposedly offset by reducing the investor's personal discount rate from 12% to 4% as well.

But now let's value a one-year stock call option contract for a share that is currently selling for $100 when the strike price is $105. Using explicit assumptions, the $100 share is expected to be selling for $100 x 1.12 = $112 at the end of the year. Thus, the stock call option is expected to generate a $7 payoff. Discounting this $7 at 12% interest (this means that you divide the $7 by 1.12) yields a current value for the option of $6.25.

Now using the implicit assumptions, the $100 share is expected to be selling for $100 x 1.04 = $104 at the end of the year. Thus, the stock call option is expected to be worthless, as the end-of-year stock price will be less than the strike price for the option contract. Discounting this $0 at 4% interest yields a current value for the option of $0. Oops! $6.25 and $0 are not quite the same number. This implicit assumption line of reasoning falls a bit short.

In 1998 and 1999 I served as the Chairman of the Pension Committee of the Actuarial Standards Board. During that time I helped draft an Actuarial Standard of Practice that specifically precludes the use of implicit assumptions. The use was precluded because of the potential for unintended consequences exactly like what is shown in the illustration above. Pension actuaries are required to use explicit assumptions when doing their work, unless any deviation is completely and fully disclosed.

HOW THE SUBSTITUTION OCCURRED

Finally, many people will be curious as to how the substitution of the risk-free rate for a more realistic expected rate of return on the underlying security occurred. To answer this question, you need to have a crystal ball. Literally, you really do need to have a crystal ball, a very special crystal ball! This crystal ball tells you whether the share price of any given stock will grow faster or slower than the risk-free rate of return over the next 30 days. If you ask it about Stock A, and the share price of Stock A will actually grow at a rate that is greater than the risk-free rate, the crystal ball glows green. If you ask it about Stock B, and the share price of Stock B will actually grow at a rate that is less than the risk-free rate, the crystal ball glows red.

Having such a crystal ball would make you very, very rich. If you ask the ball about Stock A and the ball glows green, then you borrow money from the bank at the risk-free rate in order to buy shares of Stock A with your borrowed money. Then in 30 days' time you sell your shares, pay off your loan, and put the rest of the money in your pocket. You entered the market with no money, and leave with cash in your pocket.

If you ask the crystal ball about Stock B and the ball glows red, then you sell shares of Stock B short and invest the proceeds from the short sale at the risk-free rate at the bank. Then in 30 days' time you close out your bank account, use the proceeds to make good on the shares of stock you sold short, and put the rest of the money in your pocket. You again entered the market with no money and leave with cash in your pocket.

If such a crystal ball existed, the share price of all stocks would soon be forced into growing at only the risk-free rate of return. If any stock deviated from this course, a horde of clever investors could use the crystal ball to make guaranteed gains, thus forcing the deviant stock back into line. Clearly, no such crystal ball exists, and actual stock returns that are different from the risk-free rate of return occur all the time. Investors are certainly welcome to take the indicated hedged positions, but these hedged positions involve significant risk. An investor who makes the wrong hedging strategy winds up with a loss.

Yet it is exactly these two hedged positions, either borrowing at the risk-free rate in order to buy shares or selling shares short in order to invest risk-free, that are assumed to constitute an arbitrage potential during the development of the Black-Scholes formula. When Dr. Black and Dr. Scholes assume that a clever investor (they refer to him as a speculator in their 1973 paper) can make an arbitrage gain, they are substituting the risk-free rate of return for both the true expected rate of return on the underlying security and the investor's discount rate.

Not only does this create the problems shown above with the use of implicit assumptions, but it also excludes the possibility that an investor's personal discount rate may be different from the expected rate of return on the underlying security. Given the risk involved in stock option investing, it would not be surprising to see an investor's personal discount rate that is somewhat larger than the expected rate of return on the under-lying security.

SUMMARY

Myth 5 has often been described as being surprising. It is a myth that lots of people doubted should be true, but one that has become accepted over time. But when one does the type of analysis that Dave and Deana did, the closeness of the matches confirms that the expected rate of return on the underlying se-curity is an important variable in option pricing; it is just that the Black-Scholes formula sets this variable at the risk-free rate of return. The Black-Scholes formula estimates option prices under the assumption that the underlying security has an ex-pected rate of return that is equal to the risk-free rate of return. Potential option investors who do not agree with this assump-tion, or those who have a personal discount rate different from the expected rate of return on the underlying security need to be very wary of using the Black-Scholes formula for guidance when making an option investment decision.

Nicholas Copernicus Makes His Presentation

Chapter 9

MYTH 6: OPTION MARKETS EXIST AT ALL DURATIONS AND STRIKE PRICES

A scholar named Nick Copernicus

had a theory to state for the curious.

But students that day

would rather just play.

They didn't think Nick was that serious.

MYTH 6: OPTION MARKETS EXIST AT ALL DURATIONS AND STRIKE PRICES

In the mathematical development of stock option pricing models in modern finance, it is common to use variables such as t to represent the duration of the option, S to represent the current selling price, and K to represent the strike price. Often in such developments there are no restrictions placed on the variables, such as the duration variable t must be 6 months or less. This means that the option pricing model is designed to describe reasonable option prices at all durations and strike prices. The myth-busting exercise for this chapter will be to show that there are some potential option markets, particularly for longer-term options, where the option market simply cannot exist. The conflict between the competing market forces that affect the pricing of stock option contracts is impossible to resolve.

THE IMPORTANCE OF LONGER-DURATION OPTION ESTIMATES

The statement of Myth 6 about option pricing models being appropriate for all durations and strike prices holds true for the Black-Scholes model as well. In theory, the Black-Scholes model is also designed to produce reasonable option prices at all durations and at all strike prices. Because of this fact, the Black-Scholes formula has been widely used to disclose the value of longer-term employee stock option awards for financial reporting purposes under Financial Accounting Standard 123R (FAS 123R). Rather than estimating a "price" of a listed stock option contract, when used for FAS 123R purposes, the Black-Scholes model is placing a value on the grant of an employee stock option award. This value gets disclosed in the company's annual report and affects the company's financial performance for the year.

Employee stock option awards offer an employee the right to purchase shares of stock in his or her own company at a fixed price at some point in the future. If the company's financial performance causes the stock price to grow, the employee stock option award could become very valuable for the employee. This particular usage of the Black-Scholes formula (for the purpose of valuing employee stock option awards) has brought a high level of complaint from many affected companies. This complaint was particularly strong in the high-tech sector where companies have relied heavily on employee stock options as a significant portion of key employees' compensation packages. The complaints of these companies are certainly well-founded. In spite of its storied history, and as shown in Chapter 6, the Black-Scholes model is now widely acknowledged to have serious accuracy problems.

A major step in resolving concerns about an appropriate value for employee stock option awards under FAS 123R will be to recognize that in some situations it might not be possible to have an "option market." These are situations where the conflicts between the market forces affecting the prices of option contracts are simply impossible to resolve. In these situations since it is impossible to have an option market, it will be impossible to calculate a true "market value" for the employee stock option award.

Recognizing that these situations can occur and adopting reasonable disclosure values specifically designed to meet FAS 123R requirements in these situations will go a long way toward solving the objections of concerned employers. This may have an added benefit to employees of firms that have recently cut back their stock option award programs; these companies may turn once again to employee stock options as a reasonable basis for compensating key employees.

THE NON-EXISTENCE OF
STOCK OPTION MARKETS

As noted in the previous chapter, Dave and Deana from Denver studied the idea of investing in stock options by looking at a 10-year stock put option and a 10-year stock call option on the Ibbotson large company stock index. The key specifics of the contracts were a current index of $3,246 and a strike price of $4,579. Using reasonable assumptions, Dave and Deana calculated the Black-Scholes value of either the put option contract or the call option contract to be $680. The Black-Scholes option prices bothered Dave and Deana enough that they did the extra research necessary to find out exactly how the Black-Scholes prices are determined.

As part of that process Dave compared the $680 Black-Scholes put option price with the historical average payoff of $84 for the put option contract described above. He concluded that the Black-Scholes value seemed way too big. He imagined that he was in a room full of people who were interested in making a put option investment. These people would have the choice of either buying or selling this particular 10-year put option contract on the Ibbotson large company stock index. He just didn't believe that the price of $680 would attract an equal number of willing buyers and sellers, given that the historical average payoff has only been $84. He reasoned that there would clearly be a lot more interested sellers of the contract than there would be buyers. He expected that this dynamic would put downward pressure on the $680 stock put option price.

Deana, on the other hand, studied the call option contract, which also had a Black-Scholes price of $680. She concluded that while there would be downward pressure in the case of the price of the put option contract, the opposite dynamic would be affecting the price of the $680 call option contract. In this case the room full of people would have the choice of either buying or selling this particular 10-year call option contract where the historical payoff has been $5,733. She just didn't believe that the price of $680 would attract an equal number of willing buyers and sellers. Deana reasoned that there would clearly be a lot more interested buyers of the contract than there would be sellers. She expected this dynamic would put upward pressure on the $680 stock call option price.

Yet, Dave and Deana both knew that these two different 10-year option contracts would have to have prices that were about the same number because of the possibility of a true arbitrage opportunity known as put-call parity. Unlike hedged equity trading (Myth 4), put-call parity is a very real arbitrage opportunity that does have the ability to move option markets. For the curious, put-call parity is described in Appendix 4.

When looking at these particular 10-year option contracts, it seemed to Dave and Deana that the price of the call contract needs to be way larger than the $680 Black-Scholes value in order to have an equal number of willing buyers and sellers want to engage in a transaction involving the call option contract. On the other hand, the price of the put contract needs to be way less than the $680 Black-Scholes value in order to have an equal number of willing buyers and sellers want to engage in a transaction involving the put option contract. Yet the price of each contract needs to be the same number in order to satisfy the important put-call parity arbitrage requirement. They can see no resolution to this inherent conflict. They believe that it simply would not be possible for this particular 10-year option market to exist.

To confirm their suspicions Dave and Deana tried to purchase actual 10-year stock option contracts that might be listed on the current option exchanges. They learned that no such option contracts were available. For example, there were no listed 10-year option contracts on the S&P 500 Index or other similar index. Thus, their conclusion that it would not be mathematically possible to have such an option market was strongly supported by the option market itself.

THE OPTION PRICING DILEMMA

In thinking some more about option pricing, Dave and Deana looked back at the work that they did, which was shown in the prior chapter. There they learned that the Black-Scholes formula really values the discounted expected payoff from an option contract. But when the Black-Scholes formula is used in this fashion, the investment return parameter needs to be the expected rate of return on the underlying security, not the risk-free rate of return.

As an illustration of this point, Dave considered the $84 historical average payoff on the 10-year put option contract that he had been studying. When this $84 average payoff is discounted for 10 years at a 12.26% discount rate, the discounted value becomes $26. Dave thought that a rational investor with a personal discount rate of 12.26% might be willing to pay $26 for the 10-year put option contract. It seemed to Dave that the price of $26 might be at about the right level to actually have a market in 10-year put options, whereas the Black-Scholes value of $680 seems way too large.

It turns out that a different "Black-Scholes" value of this put option contract is $25, a number close to the $26 actual discounted value of the historical payoff. But to get this particular "Black-Scholes" value, Dave needs to use 12.26% instead of the risk-free rate of return in the Black-Scholes formula. Dave needs to use a realistic expected rate of return for the underlying security instead of the risk-free rate of return. But if he does this, he seems to get put option prices that actually stand a chance of meeting market demand.

As a second illustration of this point, Deana considered the $5,733 historical average payoff on the 10-year call option contract that she had been studying. When this $5,733 average payoff is discounted for 10 years at a 12.26% discount rate, the discounted value becomes $1,804. Deana thought that a rational investor with a personal discount rate of 12.26% might be willing to pay $1,804 for this 10-year call option contract. It seemed to Deana that the price of $1,804 might be at about the right level to actually have a market in 10-year call options, whereas the Black-Scholes value of $680 seems way too small.

It turns out that a different "Black-Scholes" value of this call option contract is $1,829, a number close to the $1,804 actual discounted value of the historical payoff. But to get this particular "Black-Scholes" value, Deana needs to use 12.26% instead of the risk-free rate of return in the Black-Scholes formula. She needs to use a realistic expected rate of return for the underlying security instead of the risk-free rate of return. But if she does this, she seems to get call option prices that actually stand a chance of meeting market demand.

To verify that this same dynamic works for options with other strike prices, Dave and Deana prepared Table 19 below. This table compares the discounted value of actual Ibbotson large company stock option payoffs based on a historical development with the "Black-Scholes" values. However, in the table below, the investment return parameter is no longer the risk-free rate of return, but is instead the 12.26% actual arithmetic mean of calendar year returns for the Ibbotson Index.

Table 19

DISCOUNTED HISTORICAL PAYOFFS COMPARED WITH BLACK-SCHOLES VALUES BLACK-SCHOLES VALUES USE A 12.26% "RISK-FREE" RATE OF RETURN

Selling Price: $3,246
Risk-Free Return: 12.26%
Option Term: 10 Years
Volatility: 16%

Strike Price	Stock *Put* Option Contracts			Stock *Call* Option Contracts		
	Actual Historical Payoff	Discounted Historical Payoff	Black-Scholes Value	Actual Historical Payoff	Discounted Historical Payoff	Black-Scholes Value
$4,000.00	$41.00	$13.00	$12.00	$6,269.00	$1,972.00	$1,999.00
4,579.00	84.00	26.00	25.00	5,733.00	1,804.00	1,829.00
6,000.00	266.00	84.00	89.00	4,494.00	1,414.00	1,447.00
8,000.00	871.00	274.00	281.00	3,099.00	975.00	1,009.00
10,000.00	1,852.00	583.00	590.00	2,080.00	654.00	689.00

All in all the Black-Scholes formula works pretty well when it is used in this way to value expected option contract payoffs. Based on this analysis, Dave and Deana concluded that an estimate of a call option price or a put option price that would likely bring willing buyers and sellers together in the market should be the Black-Scholes formula for an option estimate, but with the risk-free rate of return replaced with a true expected rate of return on the underlying security.

Dave and Deana saw a very big problem. They realized that the single investment return variable in the Black-Scholes formula needs to be the expected rate of return on the underlying security in order to produce option prices that would come close to meeting the market demands of willing buyers and sellers. But using the formula in this fashion yields put and call option prices that would permit put-call parity arbitrage.

Replacing this parameter with the risk-free rate will produce a price for the put option and a price for the call option that will satisfy put-call parity but at longer durations hopelessly miss the kinds of prices that would encourage willing buyers and sellers to enter into contracts. Clearly the single investment return parameter in the Black-Scholes formula cannot be both the risk-free rate and the expected return rate for the underlying security at the same time.

MARKETS THAT EXIST

Vibrant shorter-term stock option markets obviously exist. This is because when one is dealing with shorter-term options, the impact of the investment return parameter problem discussed above is relatively small when compared with the impact of the volatility parameter. In short, there is enough "wiggle room" to produce option prices that will meet all the competing forces that affect option pricing. Investors in the stock put option market will likely be using slightly different assumptions than investors in the stock call option market, and investors are likely to have varying assumptions for the discount rate, expected rate of return on the underlying security, and volatility. This range of assumptions allows for the existence of option markets at shorter durations.

To illustrate how this works, consider a three-month put or call option on the Ibbotson Large Company Stock Index when risk-free rates are 3.5%, the selling price is the January

1, 2008, value of $3,246, and the strike price is $3,274. At this strike price, put-call parity dictates that both the put option and the call option have the same price. The final critical assumption is volatility. While 16% and 16.8% have both been used previously as reasonable volatility estimates for the Ibbotson Large Company Stock Index, no one knows for sure what future volatility will be. Some potential option contract investors might view a volatility assumption as low as 12% as being reasonable, while others might prefer a volatility assumption as high as 24% for the particular three-month duration of this option contract.

Using this 12% to 24% range for the volatility assumption then provides a range of possible put option prices and a range of possible call option prices that would allow willing buyers and sellers to consider engaging in actual transactions. Depending upon the various investors' expectations, a call option price somewhere between $114 and $189 might reasonably be expected to meet market demands on the call option contract, and a put option price between $50 and $123 might reasonably be expected to meet market demands on the put option contract.

Since these ranges overlap, it is possible to find a single price somewhere in the range of $114 to $123 that would then satisfy both the market demand requirements and put-call parity at the same time. Note that any number in this range is a possible price for both the put and call option contracts. Factors such as the investor's personal discount rate and the investor's expected rate of return on the underlying security could impact which number in that range actually emerges as the trading price for both contracts.

THE BLACK-SCHOLES OPTION PRICE FOR MARKETS THAT EXIST

It is interesting to note that the Black-Scholes value for either the put option or the call option using a 3.5% risk-free rate of return and an18% volatility assumption is $117, a number that is in the $114 to $123 range. Thus, it might be possible to have a market that exists using the $117 Black-Scholes value. However, it is important to keep in mind that there are really three different $117 numbers: a put option value, a call option value, and a Black-Scholes value.

The put option $117 number is in the put option range of $50 to $123. It represents the discounted expected payoff on the option contract, assuming that the Ibbotson Index has an expected return of 12.26%, the investor's personal discount rate is 12.26%, and the expected volatility over this particular three-month period is 23.0%.

The call option $117 number is in the call option range of $114 to $189. It represents the discounted expected payoff on the option contract, assuming that the Ibbotson Index has an expected return of 12.26%, the investor's personal discount rate is 12.26%, and the expected volatility over this particular three-month period is 12.5%.

The Black-Scholes $117 is in both ranges. It represents the expected payoff on the option contracts assuming that the Ibbotson Index has an expected rate of return of 3.5%, that an investor's personal discount rate is 3.5%, and that volatility over this particular three- month period is 18%. These three different $117 numbers arrived at in three different ways are part of a vibrant market in listed stock option contracts.

MARKETS THAT DO NOT EXIST

Now consider a 10-year put option and a 10-year call option on the Ibbotson Large Company Stock Index when risk-free rates are 3.5%, the selling price is the January 1, 2008, value of $3,246, and the strike price is $4,579. At this strike price, put-call parity dictates that both the put option and the call option have the same price. But using the same reasonable range for a volatility assumption of from 12% to 24%, the call option price range that might meet market demand is $1,810 to $1,919 and the put option price range that might meet market demand $5 to $114. These ranges are not anywhere close to having an overlap. There is no single number, not even the Black-Scholes value of $680, which has any chance of satisfying all the various forces that affect option pricing at the same time.

For longer-term options, the market simply cannot exist. Even significant ranges in reasonable assumptions will not be enough to allow option prices that would satisfy the three competing market forces: a price that would meet market demand for the put option, a price that would meet market demand for the call option, and prices that would satisfy put-call parity. Again, this "theoretical" non-existence is confirmed by the actual non-existence of longer-term listed option contracts with characteristics similar to those described in the illustrations. The markets do not exist because it is mathematically impossible for them to do so.

LONGER-TERM PRODUCT TESTING

One of the amazing aspects of Myth 6 is that it could have been busted long before now. Accuracy problems with the Black-Scholes model are now well-documented. The model is continually "product tested" by comparing the estimated stock option prices determined by the model with actual option prices. These are the prices that willing buyers and sellers use to engage in actual stock option transactions on the listed option exchanges. The model just does not seem to be doing a good job of replicating actual quotations. But the concept of "product testing" could have been explored more fully at the time the original paper was published.

While product testing by comparing model output with actual quotations occurs on an ongoing basis, there is a different kind of product testing that could have been undertaken in 1973 at the time that Dr. Black and Dr. Scholes published their original paper. This product testing would have involved using historical data to see how an actual investor would have fared had he or she used the formula to engage in an actual option transaction.

For example, it is possible to use the Ibbotson Large Company Stock Index to see how various investors might have fared had they used the Black-Scholes formula to buy option contracts. The Ibbotson Large Company Stock Index was $3.965 on January 1, 1946. This number could serve as the current selling price of the underlying security. If the option term is set at 10 years, and the strike price is set at $4.420, the Black-Scholes price for a stock put option becomes $0.79 and the Black-Scholes price for a stock call option also becomes $0.79. As in previous illustrations, the particular strike price was selected so that both the call option and put option prices would be the same.

It is then possible to see how an investor might have fared had he or she purchased either of the two options for the estimated $0.79 price. The Ibbotson Large Company Stock Index at the end of the 10-year option term was $18.561. The stock call option turned out to be a fantastic investment. The $0.79 price would have generated a payoff of $14.141 ten years later, as this number is the difference between the index value of $18.561 on January 1, 1956, and the strike price of $4.420. The average annual return (geometric mean) on this stock call option investment was 33%.

On the other hand the stock put option investment turned out to be a complete bust. Since the actual index at the end of the term exceeded the strike price by a large amount, the stock put option would have been worthless. The investor in the stock put option would have lost his or her entire investment. This represents a 100% loss.

Table 20 below illustrates the historical returns that would have been achieved had an investor purchased a 10-year stock put or stock call option contract on the Ibbotson Large Company Stock Index that appears in the *SBBI Yearbook*. The particular years included in the table were selected because they were all of the ten-year periods following World War II that would have been available as a data source at the time that Dr. Black and Dr. Scholes published their paper.

The price of each contract was determined using the Black-Scholes stock option pricing model. The risk-free rate of return was estimated to be the income return rate on intermediate term government bonds as shown in the *SBBI Yearbook*, volatility was set at a reasonable 16% level, and the strike price was set at the level where the put option price and the call option price equal each other.

The particular strike price was selected because it yields put and call prices that must be identical in order to avoid the put-call parity arbitrage potential that is discussed in Appendix 4. The dollar amount of gain shown below represents the actual amount received for making the investment, and the percent-

age gain represents the average annual percentage return that
would have been earned on the investment.

Table 20

HISTORICAL RETURN ILLUSTRATION
TEN-YEAR OPTION CONTRACTS PRICED
USING THE BLACK-SCHOLES FORMULA

Year	January Index	Risk-Free Rate	Strike Price	Option Price	Put Option		Call Option	
					Gain	Percent	Gain	Percent
1946	$3.965	1.08%	$4.420	$0.79	$0.00	-100.0%	$14.141	33%
1947	3.645	1.21	4.100	0.73	0.00	-100.0	15.678	35
1948	3.853	1.56	4.500	0.77	0.00	-100.0	13.146	33
1949	4.065	1.36	4.650	0.81	0.00	-100.0	20.648	38
1950	4.829	1.39	5.550	0.96	0.00	-100.0	22.772	37
1951	6.360	1.98	7.750	1.27	0.00	-100.0	20.705	32
1952	7.888	2.19	9.830	1.58	0.00	-100.0	26.276	32
1953	9.336	2.55	12.050	1.86	0.00	-100.0	20.904	27
1954	9.244	1.60	10.850	1.85	0.00	-100.0	29.619	32
1955	14.108	2.45	18.030	2.82	0.00	-100.0	29.109	26
1956	18.561	3.05	25.180	3.71	0.00	-100.0	27.828	22
1957	19.778	3.59	28.320	3.95	0.00	-100.0	19.354	17
1958	17.646	2.93	23.660	3.52	0.00	-100.0	35.444	26
1959	25.298	4.18	38.420	5.05	0.00	-100.0	27.222	18
1960	28.322	4.15	42.900	5.66	0.00	-100.0	17.159	12
1961	28.455	3.54	40.530	5.68	0.00	-100.0	21.935	14
1962	36.106	3.73	52.420	7.21	0.00	-100.0	18.986	10
1963	32.954	3.71	47.770	6.58	0.00	-100.0	37.186	19

The above table is quite dramatic. It shows nothing but
complete 100% losses for the stock put option contracts and
large annual gains, sometimes very large, for the stock call

option contracts. Had this sort of testing been done back in 1973, perhaps the investing public would have been a bit more skeptical of the new formula.

It is noted that there have been times when relatively high risk-free rates have been followed by a very weak stock market, yielding a positive return for the Black-Scholes put option value. But as would reasonably be expected, these times have been quite rare.

THE OPTION PRICING DYNAMIC

The market forces that affect option prices make it impossible to find a single price that would satisfy both put and call option investors for longer term options when the strike level is "at the future money," the modern finance term used to describe the strike prices shown in the above illustrations where the put and call prices must equal each other. Yet to avoid put-call parity arbitrage, these types of options need to have the same price. This single number when serving as a stock put option price will be way too high, and this single number when serving as a stock call option price will be way too low when compared with prices which actually stand a chance of encouraging willing buyers and sellers to enter into transactions. In short, the option market for longer duration options at certain strike price levels simply cannot exist.

The Investor's Hard Choices

Chapter 10

CONCLUDING REMARKS

Investing is hard. The road is sure rough.

To make a sound choice is often quite tough.

To take less risk or opt for more,

finding the path is a difficult chore.

My wife and I have a friend we bicycle with from time to time. He retired when his financial planner told him that there was only a 2% chance that he would run out of money during his retirement years. He and his wife decided that at the 2% level, they would take the risk and retire. He is now working again; his financial planner tells him that the 2% chance happened.

However, if the mathematics of conditional probabilities had been used, my friend's chance of running out of money would have been calculated to be in the 15%-20% range. At this higher level, my friend would not have chosen to retire, but would have chosen to continue working. The issues addressed in this book have a very real impact on the lives of everyday investors. It is hoped that by writing this book, similar disruptions in the lives of other people can be avoided.

The publication of the book occurs at a very tumultuous time in the financial services industry:

(a) Major firms have gone out of business or needed a government-backed guarantee.

(b) It is well-known within the academic finance community that the Black-Scholes formula has serious accuracy issues.

(c) Articles in the general financial press such as *Business Week* or *The Economist* are raising concerns about problems in modern finance, especially problems associated with the proper assessment of investment risk.

(d) The Congress of the United States approved a $700 billion taxpayer-backed program to "bail out" the financial services industry.

These are symptoms of a very serious problem in modern finance. *Six Myths in Modern Finance that Every Investor Needs to Know* goes right to the root cause of this problem – the treatment of conditional data as if it were independent data. It is a book about a serious mathematical issue that contributes significantly to the current difficulties in the financial services industry.

The development of this key mathematical concern is presented in detail in the three published technical papers cited in the Introduction. Of course, the technical papers make no mention of Dave and Deana from Denver, Stu Stevens, or Carl Cantmiss. These are fictitious characters that were introduced to help bring this serious mathematical problem to the attention of the investing public. Creating the visual imagery necessary to bring complex mathematical ideas to life is the whole goal of this book. Hopefully, this goal has been accomplished.

CONTINUOUS AND DIFFERENTIABLE MATHEMATICAL FORMULAS

This appendix is used to present a mathematical demonstration that the process of accumulating wealth through stock investing can be treated as an essentially continuous mathematical function and that when the arithmetic mean is calculated from ever smaller components of this wealth accumulation, the arithmetic mean approaches the geometric mean of the original data set.

Some might argue that the wealth accumulation process must of necessity be discrete, since stocks and other assets must be valued in dollars and cents, not fractions of a penny. While this is a bit like arguing that time is discrete if one happens to be using a digital clock to measure time, there is a stronger argument that the wealth accumulation function is essentially continuous and differentiable. It is possible to create a continuous, differentiable wealth accumulation function that exactly matches any given discrete wealth accumulation function at every data point, even if the data points are only a fraction of a second apart.

Assume there exists a discrete wealth function with wealth W_i at each time t_i, $i = 1$ to N. The cubic function

$$W(t) = \frac{2(W_1 - W_2)}{(t_2 - t_1)^3} (t\text{-}t_1)^3 - \frac{3(W_1 - W_2)}{(t_2 - t_1)^2} (t\text{-}t_1)^2 + W_1$$

is continuous and differentiable at every point between t_1 and t_2. Furthermore $W(t_1) = W_1$, $W(t_2) = W_2$, $W'(t_1) = 0$, and

$W'(t_2) = 0$. The above function can be used between times t_1 and t_2 to create a continuous differentiable wealth function between the two times, such that the wealth at time t_1 is W_1 and the wealth at time t_2 is W_2. Since the derivatives at times t_1 and t_2 are both zero, a similar function can be extended from time t_2 to t_3, t_3 to t_4, t_4 to t_5, etc., continuously and still be differentiable at all time periods.

The following theorem is used to demonstrate that the arithmetic mean determined by taking smaller and smaller increments of the above function approaches the geometric mean.

Theorem: If $W(t)$ is a continuous, differentiable function that measures a given wealth at time $t(0 \le t \le n)$; and A_m is the arithmetic mean of a sample of m observations of $W(t)$, taken at equidistant intervals of length n/m; then

$$\lim_{m \to \infty} A_m = \left(\frac{W(n)}{W(0)} \right)^{1/n} , \text{ the geometric mean of the wealth.}$$

Proof:

$$\lim_{m \to \infty} A_m = \lim_{m \to \infty} \left[\frac{1}{m} \sum_{k=0}^{m-1} \frac{W\left(\frac{(k+1)n}{m}\right)}{W\left(\frac{kn}{m}\right)} \right]^{\frac{m}{n}}$$

$$= \lim_{m \to \infty} \left[\frac{1}{m} \sum_{k=0}^{m-1} \frac{W\left(\frac{kn}{m}\right) + W'\left(\frac{kn}{m}\right)\frac{n}{m}}{W\left(\frac{kn}{m}\right)} \right]^{\frac{m}{n}} , \text{ where}$$

$W'(t)$ is the derivative of $W(t)$.

$$= \lim_{m \to \infty} \left[1 + \frac{1}{m} \sum_{k=0}^{m-1} \frac{W'\left(\frac{kn}{m}\right)\frac{n}{m}}{W\left(\frac{kn}{m}\right)} \right]^{\frac{m}{n}}$$

$$= \lim_{m \to \infty} \left[1 + \frac{1}{m} \int_{0}^{n} \frac{W'(t)}{W(t)} dt \right]^{\frac{m}{n}}$$

$$= \lim_{m \to \infty} [1 + \frac{1}{m} (\ell n(W(n)) - \ell n(W(0)))]^{\frac{m}{n}}$$

$$= \lim_{m \to \infty} [1 + \ell n \left(\frac{W(n)}{W(0)} \right)^{1/n} \bullet \frac{n}{m}]^{\frac{m}{n}}$$

$$= e^{\ell n \left(\frac{W(n)}{W(o)} \right)^{1/n}} = \left(\frac{W(n)}{W(0)} \right)^{1/n} \qquad \text{Q.E.D.}$$

LOGNORMAL DISTRIBUTIONS

Investment forecasts provide investors with information about potential risks and rewards of a particular investment opportunity. In making a forecast, it is common to use historical data as a guide in selecting key forecasting variables. While past performance is no guarantee of what the future holds, with appropriate adjustment for current market conditions this historical guide does provide the user of the forecast with reasonable information that may be helpful in making investment decisions.

Investment return forecasting models found in the literature are designed to provide not just a single point estimate of future return, but a complete distribution of possible values. If it were assumed that past returns were distributed normally (fit the standard bell-shaped curve), one could use historical data to estimate the mean and standard deviation of a prospective distribution. Having this distribution would then provide answers for questions not only about the expected mean return, but about the probability that future results may exceed, or fall below, any given threshold.

It is a fact, however, that historical results have not tended to fit the traditional normal curve pattern, and a slightly different model is commonly used, the lognormal distribution model. This model is based on the fact that history has shown return relatives on stocks and other economic measures to be skewed toward the larger values. This is expected, since by the very definition of return relatives they can become quite large, but never fall below the value of zero. To compensate for this skewing, the model assumes that investment returns are lognormally distributed. This means that if r is a random variable representing rates of return measured over some fixed time frame, $1 + r$ is its return relative, and the random variable $R = \ell n (1 + r)$ is assumed to be normally distributed.

This normal distribution of logarithms is completely determined by its mean (μ) and its standard deviation (σ). Once these parameters are determined, the lognormal forecasting process may be used to provide complete distributions for all investment horizons. To show the development of these forecasts, one needs only to analyze a general lognormal density function, which is defined as follows:

$$f(x) = \frac{1}{\sigma\sqrt{2\pi}} \cdot \frac{1}{x} \cdot e^{\frac{-(\ell nx - \mu)^2}{2\sigma^2}} \tag{1}$$

The mathematical expectation, variance, and standard deviation of the random variable x are calculated to be as follows:

Expected Value: $\qquad E(x) = e^{\mu + \frac{\sigma^2}{2}}$ $\qquad\qquad$ (2)

Variance: $\qquad \sigma^2(x) = [E(x)]^2 \cdot (e^{\sigma^2} - 1)$ $\qquad$ (3)

Standard Deviation: $\qquad \sigma(x) = [E(x)] \cdot \sqrt{e^{\sigma^2} - 1}$ $\qquad$ (4)

The distribution of wealth after n time periods is given by the equation:

$$W(n)_z = e^{nu + z\sigma\sqrt{n}} \tag{5}$$

where z is the z-score of the percentile in question.

For any given time horizon, n, the wealth distribution described by equation (5) is also lognormal and has the same density function as shown in equation (1), except that the parameter μ is replaced with $n\mu$, and the parameter σ^2 is replaced with $n\sigma^2$. The expected wealth after n time periods is:

$$EW(n) = e^{\,nu + \frac{n\sigma^2}{2}} \qquad\qquad (6)$$

Once the parameters μ and σ^2 are determined, the investor can use the lognormal distribution tool to answer questions such as: What is the likelihood that a $1,000 investment will grow to exceed $10,000 after a 15-year investment period?

The only remaining issue is how to use the historical data to determine the parameters μ and σ^2. While addressing that issue, it is helpful to keep in mind the outcomes if the parameters, and the resulting lognormal model, fit ideal circumstances:

1) Different approaches to using the same historical data should produce substantially equivalent results. Thus, the forecast should depend on the data itself, and not on how a given forecaster chooses to use the data.

2) Long-term wealth projected by the model should be reasonably close to the long-term wealth that serves as the data source. If the long-term expected wealth from the model significantly exceeds or falls below the actual wealth, the investor would be receiving information on potential wealth distributions under the potentially misleading assumption that the future expected returns are either significantly better or significantly worse than what has actually been observed.

3) The expected distribution of wealth at shorter-term time horizons should bear a reasonable relationship to the actual distribution of historical results. After all, long-term wealth can only be achieved by the compounding of shorter-term val-

ues. Hence, the accuracy of the short-term distribution is essential for accurate projections of long-term wealth.

PARAMETER DETERMINATION – INDEPENDENT HISTORICAL RETURN METHOD

The most common method of parameter determination is the one described in the *SBBI Yearbook*. This method uses the arithmetic mean of a historical sampling of data and the sample standard deviation from the same data. Letting these values be $E_A(r)$ and S_A respectively, the equations for μ and σ are defined as follows:

$$\mu = \ell n\,(1 + E_A(r)) - \frac{\sigma^2}{2} \tag{7}$$

$$\sigma = \sqrt{\ell n\,\left(1 + \left(\frac{S_A}{1 + E_A\,(r)}\right)^2\right)} \tag{8}$$

These results were derived by simply setting the sample mean equal to the calculated mean:

$$E_A(1+r) = 1 + E_A(r) = e^{\mu + \frac{\sigma^2}{2}} \tag{9}$$

And by setting the sample variance equal to the calculated variance:

$$S_A{}^2 = (1 + E_A(r))^2 \cdot (e^{\sigma^2} - 1) \tag{10}$$

Equation (10) can be solved for σ, and equation (9) can be solved for μ. The solutions produce the exact values for μ and σ that were presented in equations (7) and (8) above.

Unfortunately, these equations do not yield unique results. For example, as shown in Chapter 3, the expected annual return for the Ibbotson large company stock return data ranges from 10.36% to 13.30%, just depending upon how the single 82-year large company stock return history and formulas (7) and (8) are used to determine the parameters μ and σ^2. Thus, this parameter determination process fails the first of the ideal criteria listed in the previous section. The results from any given forecast depend heavily upon how the forecaster chooses to use the data.

Also, unfortunately, for the most common ways in which the parameters are actually determined, the model fails the other two ideal criteria as well. For the Ibbotson large company stock return data, the 82-year expected wealth is $13,136 for the forecasting model developed with parameters determined from annual calendar year data, and the expected wealth is $27,980 when the parameters are determined using data with a June 30 fiscal year. Both of these results are significantly larger than the actual 82-year wealth for the Ibbotson large company stock return data of $3,246.39.

Since the long-term results are so far off, it is not surprising that the short-term expected distribution of results is also significantly different from the distribution of actual results. Chart 8 compares the distribution of expected monthly returns using the above parameter determination process with the actual distribution of returns. The expected distribution clearly has a much larger standard deviation than is present in the actual results.

The independent historical return method of parameter determination is based on a philosophy that each calculated historical return, whether it be a monthly, quarterly, or annual return, constitutes an independently determined result. Under this philosophy, the arithmetic mean of these historical results is, in fact, the best estimate for a future return. When these shorter period returns are combined to produce longer period returns through the creation of a lognormal model, it is possible to develop a distribution of long-term returns. In this case the actual long-term history that serves as the source for the data winds up near the median of the expected long-term distribution, and this median value is less than the mean of the distribution, sometimes by significant amounts. In short, this model fails all three of the ideal criteria and calls into question the basic philosophy that drives the model.

The next section of this Appendix 2 introduces a parameter determination process based on a different philosophy. This new process generates a model where the outcome is much more in line with the ideal criteria presented in the prior section.

PARAMETER DETERMINATION – CONDITIONAL PROBABILITY METHOD

The parameter determination process in the previous section was driven by the assumption that each historical result constitutes an independently determined event. In this section, a different parameter selection method is developed, one based on the assumption that the single observed long-term result should lie at the mean, not the median, of the expected long-term lognormal distribution. The monthly, quarterly, or annual returns become just periodic observations of this single long-term result.

Under this method of parameter determination, periodic historical data is used only for the purpose of determining the relationship between the parameters μ and σ^2, using equations (7) and (8) above. Once the relationship is determined, the entire long-term history is used for the purpose of calculating the exact parameter values. The interim determinations based on equations (7) and (8) are reduced proportionately, so that the final ending wealth matches the ending wealth that was actually observed. While this process still depends on the judgment of the forecaster for determining the relationship between parameters, the use of the entire long-term history for calculating final parameter values significantly reduces the differences between alternative forecasts derived from the same data.

Under the conditional probability method of parameter determination, future stock returns are also assumed to be lognormally distributed. However, the parameters in the specific forecasting model are determined by the above process. Obviously, different data sets will produce different forecasts. But as noted above, the level of variability between different forecasts is significantly reduced.

Also, the parameter determination process presented in this section meets the second ideal criteria mentioned above by its very design. Using this process, the expected long-term wealth for the model will always be the long-term wealth actually observed.

Finally, the distribution of actual historical monthly results needs to be compared with the expected distribution, as determined by the lognormal density function with parameters based on the above determination process. However, the philosophy for the revised method is that the actual long-term historical result is just a single data element from the complete distribution of long-term returns, and this single data element lies near the mean of expected long-term results. Hence, to develop an expected distribution of observed periodic results, one must first determine the conditional lognormal probability density function for the distribution of periodic results described by equation (1), given that ending wealth is at its expected value. This density function is given by the following equation:

$$c(x) = \frac{1}{x} \cdot \frac{\sqrt{n}}{\sqrt{n-1}} \cdot \frac{1}{\sigma\sqrt{2\pi}} \; e^{\left[\frac{-n(\ln x - (\mu + \frac{\sigma^2}{2}))^2}{2(n-1)\sigma^2} \right]} \tag{11}$$

Chart 10 compares the distribution of the monthly results using this density function with the actual 984 calendar month returns for the Ibbotson large company stock return data.

The difference between Charts 8 and 10 is quite dramatic. A quick visual scan of Chart 8 shows the expected standard deviation is clearly larger than what was observed in the actual history of results, whereas Chart 10 results are much more consistent with the actual historical data.

This observation is not at all surprising. The independent historical return method yields expected future returns at the arithmetic mean of actually observed historical data, whereas the conditional probability method yields expected future returns equal to the geometric mean of the actually observed data. This distinction is critical since the difference between the geometric mean and arithmetic mean is a measure of the variability of the data. If the data is uniform, the geometric mean and arithmetic mean produce the same result. If the data is not uniform, the arithmetic mean will exceed the geometric mean; and the greater the variability, the greater the difference between the means. If a forecast is based on the arithmetic mean, it counts this variability twice. The variability is fully reflected one time by the geometric mean and then reflected a second time by the difference between the geometric and arithmetic means.

While this statement seems intuitively obvious from general reasoning, it can also be demonstrated mathematically. The lognormal model yields expected wealth after n time periods as described by equation (6), which in turn yields a constant expected geometric mean return of $e^{\mu+\frac{\sigma^2}{2}}$ for all time periods. However, the expected value of the conditional probability density function in equation (11) is:

$$E_r(x) = e^{\mu + \frac{\sigma^2}{2} + \frac{(n-1)\sigma^2}{2n}} \tag{12}$$

Since the underlying returns vary from year to year, the above equation (12) shows that historically observed arithmetic means contain an extra variability component if the expected wealth described by the lognormal process is actually achieved. These larger arithmetic means do not affect the expected value of wealth, which is always given by equation (6).

THE BLACK-SCHOLES STOCK OPTION PRICING MODEL

The Black-Scholes Stock Option Pricing Model was published in 1973 in the *Journal of Political Economy* and has been considered to be a major break through in the field of option pricing. The basic model relies on five key determinants to estimate the price of the option contract: stock price, strike price, volatility, time to expiration, and short-term (risk-free) interest rate. The basic formula for a call option contract price is noted below:

$$OP_c = SN(d_1) - Ke^{-rt}N(d_2)$$

In the above formula N is the cumulative standard normal distribution, and

$$d_1 = \frac{\ln(S/K) + (r + \frac{\sigma^2}{2})t}{\sigma\sqrt{t}}$$

$$d_2 = d_1 - \sigma\sqrt{t}$$

S = the current selling price of the stock
K = the strike price
r = the risk-free rate of return
t = the time until the option needs to be exercised
σ = the volatility of the stock.

There is a parallel formula that describes the theoretical price of a put option contract. Both of the basic formulas have modifications that will reflect the impact of dividend payments.

Appendix 4

STOCK OPTION PRICING
AND ARBITRAGE

Modern finance has identified two different ways that a potential arbitrage opportunity could impact the pricing of stock option contracts. These arbitrage opportunities occur when two option contracts contain a relative pricing problem that allows one of the contracts to be pitted against the other in such a way that a clever investor can make a guaranteed gain with absolutely no risk. It is the complete absence of risk that is the hallmark of an arbitrage opportunity.

The first of these two potential arbitrage opportunities is referred to as the higher price/higher strike price opportunity. This occurs if there is an option on Stock A that has both a higher price and a higher strike price than a different option with the same term on Stock A. The second type of arbitrage opportunity is known as put-call parity. This is a fairly complex topic, but it is important and will be explained in detail below.

Both of these arbitrage opportunities are real, and they affect the prices of stock option contracts in the same way the arbitrage opportunity would affect the price of miniature footballs in the Dave and Deana example shown in Chapter 7. Neither of these two stock option arbitrage opportunities is affected by the busting of Myth 4, and stock option investors will still need to consider the impact that these arbitrage opportunities have on actual stock option prices. These two arbitrage illustrations are included in this book only to provide relevant background material.

HIGHER PRICE/HIGHER STRIKE PRICE

The first stock option arbitrage opportunity that will be discussed is known as the higher price/higher strike price arbitrage opportunity. This is a very real arbitrage opportunity, and actual option prices will change in order to be sure this opportunity does not exist. As an example of the higher price/higher strike price arbitrage opportunity, consider two different 30-day stock call options on Stock A. Stock Call Option X has a strike price of $110 and is selling for $14. Stock Call Option Y has a strike price of $115 is selling for $16. Thus, Stock Call Option Y has both a higher price and a higher strike price than Stock Call Option X.

This is a situation that the market will not allow to exist for long. A clever investor will soon realize the quick, easy way to make a sure gain. The investor first writes an option contract for Stock Call Option Y, the $115 option, which means that the buyer of the contract pays the clever investor $16. The clever investor then turns around and buys Stock Call Option X, the $110 option, for $14. So far, the clever investor has made $2 on this transaction.

Furthermore, 30 days later at the end of the option term for both options there is the potential for another gain with absolutely no downside risk of a loss. If the value of Stock A is anything less than $110, both option contracts are worthless, and the clever investor just keeps his $2. If the share price ends up at some value between $110 and $115, say $113, then the clever investor winds up making an additional $3 on Stock Call Option X, the contract that he bought, as this is the difference between the share price of $113 and the strike price of $110. He still owes nothing on the contract that he wrote, Stock Call Option Y, since the share price of $113 is still less than the strike price of $115.

Finally, if the share price is greater than $115, the clever investor uses the proceeds from the contract he bought to make the payout in the contract he wrote, netting an additional $5 gain at the end of the 30-day period. More specifically, if the price of Stock A is $150 at the end of the 30-day option term, the clever investor makes $40 on the contract he bought, Stock Call Option X, as this is the difference between the share price of $150 and the strike price for this option of $110. But he only has to spend $35 to make good on the contract he wrote, Stock Call Option Y, as this is the difference between the share price of $150 and the strike price for this option of $115. The clever investor pockets the $5 difference.

The clever investor makes from $2 to $7 with no risk whatsoever. This type of arbitrage is a very real force in option pricing. The option market simply will not allow a situation exhibited by Stock Call Options X and Y to exist for long. Either the price of Stock Call Option X will increase, or the price of Stock Call Option Y will decrease, or both will happen. But the arbitrage opportunity will be closed. Note that the clever investor knew exactly what to do to take advantage of this arbitrage opportunity. There were no assumptions that needed to be made, and there was absolutely no risk that the clever investor would suffer a loss. Just to repeat one more time: it is the complete absence of risk that makes this transaction an arbitrage opportunity.

PUT-CALL PARITY

There is a second type of arbitrage that can occur in stock option pricing that is equally important, referred to as put-call parity arbitrage. This arbitrage opportunity also has a very real effect on option prices. This type of arbitrage opportunity exists when certain stock put option prices and certain stock call option prices on the same underlying security get out of whack with each other. Either these prices get too far apart or they get too close together. Although the illustration of this point is complex, it is included in this book because the issue is quite important.

The first step is to identify what it means to have a stock call option price and a stock put option price get out of whack with each other. After all, "out of whack" is not the most precise of mathematical terms. The key features that create the potential for a put-call parity arbitrage opportunity are that there is a stock call option and a stock put option with the same duration and same strike price on the same underlying security.

The potential for a put-call parity problem will first be described in words, just so you have a formal statement of the problem. This formal statement will be followed with an illustration of a situation where a put-call parity problem exists. Finally, it will be shown how a clever investor can take advantage of a put-call parity problem to make a guaranteed return with absolutely no risk of loss.

Checking to see if there is a put-call parity problem is a three-step process. The formal description of this process is as follows:

(1) The first step in checking to see if there is put-call parity problem is to subtract the price of the put option contract from the price of the call option contract.

(2) The second step is to then subtract the strike price discounted at the risk-free rate of return from the current selling price of the underlying stock.

(3) The third step is to compare the numbers. If these two numbers are not reasonably close to one another, then the put-call parity arbitrage opportunity exists. In other words, if these two numbers are not reasonably close to one another, the put and call prices are "out of whack."

As stated before, put-call parity is a complex process. The following illustration is an example of a put-call parity arbitrage opportunity, and it is included to show how important put-call parity is to the entire option pricing dynamic. Consider the illustration of one-year stock call and stock put options on Stock A where the selling price of the underlying Stock A is $110.00 per share, the strike price of both the put option contract and the call option contract is $105.00, and the risk-free rate of return is 8%. The stock call option is selling for $30, and the stock put option is selling for $15.

The basic essentials for a put-call parity problem are all in place. There is a single underlying security, Stock A, which has both stock put options and stock call options available. Furthermore these options have the same term, one-year, and the same strike price, $105. All of these basics must be in place for the possible put-call parity problem to occur.

To see if the problem actually exists, however, requires putting numbers with the formal verbal description of the put-call parity arbitrage opportunity.

(1) The first step is to subtract the price of the put option from the price of the call option. This result is $30 - $15 = $15. $15 is the first number.

(2) The first part of the second step is to calculate a number described as "the strike price discounted at the risk-free rate of return." To get this answer, one takes the strike price and divides it by the number 1 plus the discount rate. In this case the divisor becomes 1.08, and "the strike price discounted at the risk-free rate of return" becomes $105.00/(1.08) = $97.22. This number is critical since this represents the amount of money that a clever investor could borrow from a bank at 8% interest and be assured of paying back exactly $105.00 at the end of the year. This loan repayment would consist of a $97.22 principle

payment and a payment of $7.78 to reflect interest for the one year that the clever investor had the loan. Once "the strike price discounted at the risk-free rate of return" has been determined, it is possible to calculate the second number in the put-call parity verbal description. For this illustration the second number, the selling price minus the strike price discounted at the risk-free rate of return, becomes $110.00 - $97.22 or $12.78.

(3) The third step is to compare the two numbers. In this case, one number is $15, and the other number is $12.78. Hence, the arbitrage opportunity exists.

Knowing that the potential for an arbitrage opportunity exists and knowing what to do about it are two different things. The above presentation says only that a potential exists, but it does not say anything about what a clever investor needs to do to take advantage of the arbitrage opportunity or give any indication of how much "free money" the clever investor could make from this type of arbitrage. Unfortunately, taking advantage of the arbitrage opportunity is not nearly as easy as the simple steps that Dave and Deana needed to take with regard to the miniature football opportunity described in Chapter 7.

In the case of this particular put-call parity situation, a clever investor would engage in four separate transactions:

1. Write the stock call option.
2. Borrow the discounted strike price.
3. Buy a share of stock.
4. Buy the stock put option.

This process is complex, but the potential payback for a clever investor is quite large. So it is worth the effort to work through the details.

By writing (selling) the call option, the clever investor receives $30, the price of the call option contract. When this is added to the $97.22, the discounted strike price that the clever investor borrows from the bank, the clever investor now has $127.22 to spend. He first uses $110 to purchase a share of the underlying stock and then uses $15 to buy the put option. Thus, the clever investor has $2.22 left over. Hopefully he won't spend it all at once!

The important thing is that the clever investor entered this process with absolutely no money and now has $2.22 in his pocket. Since these numbers seem on the small side, consider what happens if each of these numbers is multiplied by 1,000,000, and the process involves options on a million shares of stock. Now, the clever investor entered the process with no money, but has $2,220,000 in his pocket. This arbitrage opportunity thing can generate some pretty big payoffs.

Finally, it is important to consider what happens at the end of the year and all the various commitments made under the option contracts need to be settled up. First consider the case where the actual ending share price on the underlying security is something less than $105, say $80. In this situation, the clever investor owes nothing on the stock call option that he wrote, but he makes $25 on the stock put option that he bought. He will also get $80 by selling the one share of stock that he bought. Adding this $80 to the $25 he made on the put contract, he now has $105. This is the exact amount that he needs to pay off his bank loan. The clever investor gets to keep the $2.22, or $2,220,000 in the case of the larger transaction. Not a bad year's work.

But what happens if the price of the stock at the end of the year is something larger than $105, say $150? In this situation, the put option contract is worthless, but the clever investor needs to make good on the stock call option that he wrote. In this case the person who bought the stock call option will now want his $45, which is the difference between the strike price in the option contract and the current price of the underlying stock. But the clever investor merely sells the share of stock that he originally bought for $110 at its now current price of $150. This generates the exact amount that he needs to pay the $45 he owes on the stock call option contract and the $105 he owes to pay off the bank loan. The clever investor still gets to keep the $2.22, or $2,220,000 in the case of the larger transaction. Again, not a bad year's work.

It is critical to note that the clever investor entered the market with absolutely no money and was able to leave with a sizeable gain no matter what happened to the share price of the underlying shares. This again is a real arbitrage opportunity, as long as the transaction costs are less than the potential gain. The option market will not allow this kind of opportunity to exist. Either the price of the call option will come down a bit, or the price of the put option will go up a bit, or there may be some movement in both option prices. But whatever happens, the opportunity for put-call parity arbitrage will be eliminated by the stock option market.

These two illustrations show just how important arbitrage is in the pricing of stock options. The potential gain for a clever investor is so significant that the market will adjust so as to close the arbitrage opportunity. In each of the above cases, the investor could make the return with absolutely no risk whatsoever. There were no assumptions to make about the future market; the clever investor merely needed to take several well- defined administrative steps. Just to repeat it one more time: it is this absence of risk that is essential for an arbitrage opportunity to exist.

THE RISK-FREE
RATE SUBSTITUTION

This appendix presents the details of the mathematical demonstration that shows that the risk-free rate of return gets substituted for the expected rate of return on the underlying security in the Black-Scholes option pricing model.

Before considering the role of arbitrage avoidance, it is relatively natural to see that the value of a stock option might depend on the distribution of anticipated changes in the value of the stock. For example, for a call option if there is a relatively high probability that the stock price will grow to exceed the strike price, or even a small, but significant, probability that the stock price will grow to exceed the strike price by a large amount, the option clearly appears to have more value than if there is a high probability the share price will always remain below the strike price, or if in those instances where the share price is expected to exceed the strike price, the excess is relatively small.

The first step in this demonstration is to calculate for any given time horizon, t, the expected distribution of returns on the underlying security. Assuming that returns are lognormally distributed (the Black-Scholes assumption), and letting x be a given return relative, the lognormal density function that describes this distribution is as follows:

$$f(x) = \frac{1}{\sigma\sqrt{2\pi}\sqrt{t}} \; \frac{1}{x} \; e^{\frac{-(\ln x - ut)^2}{2\sigma^2 t}} \tag{1}$$

The second step is to calculate the expected future share value, given an initial share value of S. But this is simply Sx, or the initial share value multiplied by the appropriate rate of growth in stock value.

The third step will be to calculate the potential gain from a call option, assuming that the gain in the stock price of x is actually achieved. If the strike price is K, then the theoretical gain from the stock call option is Sx-K, for any return, x, that is greater than K/S.

The fourth step is to calculate the theoretical gain from the stock call option. This is the probability weighted summation of all possible Sx-K gains, and is given by the formula:

$$\int_{K/S}^{\infty} (Sx - K) \frac{1}{\sigma\sqrt{2\pi}\sqrt{t}} \frac{1}{x} e^{\frac{-(\ln x - ut)^2}{2\sigma^2 t}} dx \tag{2}$$

Finally, since the above expression represents the expected gain at the end of the option expiration period, the theoretical stock call option price is then just the discounted value of the above expected gain using an appropriate discount rate, g. Thus, the theoretical stock call option price is given by the following equation:

$$OP_c = e^{-gt} \int_{K/S}^{\infty} (Sx - K) \frac{1}{\sigma\sqrt{2\pi}\sqrt{t}} \frac{1}{x} e^{\frac{-(\ln x - ut)^2}{2\sigma^2 t}} dx \tag{3}$$

While formula (3) seems relatively complex, an interesting development occurs if the assumed annual discount rate, g, is set equal to the expected annual rate of return for the underlying security, which is just the expected value for the distribution of returns described by the density function, f(x), in equation (1). The equality between these two rates is expressed as follows:

$$g = \mu + \frac{\sigma^2}{2} \tag{4}$$

In this case, the theoretical stock call option price as described by formula (3) becomes:

$$OP_c = SN(d_1) - Ke^{-gt}N(d_2) \qquad (5)$$

In the above formula N is the cumulative standard normal distribution, and

$$d_1 = \frac{\ln(S/K) + (g + \frac{\sigma^2}{2})t}{\sigma\sqrt{t}} \qquad (6)$$

$$d_2 = d_1 - \sigma\sqrt{t} \qquad (7)$$

The basic layout of this formula is similar to the formula that appears in Black-Scholes Option Pricing Model. The theoretical development presented in this section is somewhat different from the presentation offered by Black and Scholes in their 1973 paper. It emphasizes the importance of equation (4) in the valuation of stock options when using a formula such as the Black-Scholes formula. Given that Black and Scholes derived the option pricing formula by a different approach, the importance of equation (4) appears not to have been addressed.

There is an exactly parallel development for the theoretical price of a stock put option. In this case equation (4) plays the same important role, and the theoretical stock put option price is given by:

$$OP_p = SN(d_1) - Ke^{-gt}N(d_2) - (S-Ke^{-gt}) \qquad (8)$$

where d_1, and d_2 are defined exactly as described above.

The theoretical option pricing model, as developed so far, appears to generate formulae similar to those in the Black-Scholes Option Pricing Model. It uses similar inputs to the Black-

Scholes model, but with one key difference – the discount rate, g, and the lognormal distribution parameters, μ and σ, must be selected with due regard for equation (4) in order for the formula to be algebraically correct. In the Black-Scholes model the discount rate is set at the risk-free rate, which would usually be somewhat lower than the expected rate of return on the underlying security,

$$\mu + \frac{\sigma^2}{2}.$$

A key advantage to the theoretical development presented above is that it clearly emphasizes that in option pricing that would induce a willing buyer and willing seller to enter into the transaction there is a relationship between the discount parameter, g, and the volatility measure σ. If each of these parameters is calculated independently, this relationship could be lost, causing the option valuation results to be skewed. It is noted here that the risk-free rate of return and arbitrage avoidance are critical elements of option pricing and need to be addressed.

This still leaves open the important question of calculating the lognormal parameters, μ and σ, from historical data. The Black-Scholes Option Pricing Model assumes that historical returns may be treated as independent events for statistical analysis purposes. It calculates σ as the standard deviation of the logarithms of a sampling of historical returns.

However, using conditional probabilities, the parameters μ and σ² as determined under traditional calculation processes are reduced proportionately until the expected return for the lognormal distribution is equal to the expected long-term geometric mean return for the underlying security. Letting g be the long-term expected geometric mean, using conditional probabilities, g is simultaneously equal to the expected discount rate and the expected lognormal parameter μ, as calculated under the traditional calculation process for a very large sampling of historical data. These relationships dictate the proportional reduction so that the new volatility parameter, v, is described as follows:

$$v = \sqrt{\frac{2g\sigma^2}{2g + \sigma^2}} \tag{9}$$

where σ is defined as the standard deviation of the logarithms of a set of historical returns. Determining the volatility parameter, v, in this fashion and using it in lieu of σ in the basic option pricing formulae always assures that the relationship between the expected return and expected volatility as described by equation (4) holds true.

It is not possible to discuss stock option pricing without discussing the importance of the risk-free interest rate and the put-call parity theorem. The put-call parity theorem states that for a given strike price, the difference between an actual call price and an actual put price must equal the difference between the current share price of the underlying security and the strike price discounted at the risk-free rate of return. If this equation does not hold, the situation leads to an arbitrage opportunity providing a guaranteed return for the investor.

In the theoretical development presented so far, the relationship between call and put prices fails the put-call parity theorem; thus, one or both of the above theoretical option prices need to be adjusted so that this theorem holds true.

The put-call parity theorem and the use of the risk-free rate of return only address the difference between a given put price and a given call price, not their specific values. For example, the put-call parity theorem may dictate that the difference between two given prices be $5, but it does not specify whether the actual prices are $20 and $25, $24 and $29, or some other pair of prices whose difference is $5. Thus, the theoretical development presented above is still a critical element of option pricing.

By examining empirical data, it is evident that for strike prices somewhat below the current stock price, the put option branch of the theoretical formula presented above tends to match actual put option prices. In this situation when the theoretical call option prices are adjusted to comply with the put-call parity theorem, they also match actual call option prices.

However, at strike prices somewhat above the current stock price, the reverse is true. At the higher strike prices, the call option branch of the theoretical formula presented above tends to match actual call option prices. And once again when the theoretical put option prices are adjusted to comply with the put-call parity theorem, they, too, match actual put option prices.

These results are exactly what would be expected. For relatively low strike prices, the theoretical put option price approaches zero. Thus, it is not possible to adjust the theoretical put option prices, and any adjustments must be made to the call option formula. For relatively high strike prices, the reverse is true, since at high strike prices the call option prices approach zero.

The problems presented by put-call parity may be addressed by using linear interpolation. In other words, use the theoretical prices developed above over the strike price ranges where the theoretical prices are accurate, but use linear interpolation to determine option prices at other strike price levels. The above demonstration shows the role that the expected rate of return can play in option pricing, and demonstrates that the Black-Scholes formula substitutes the risk-free rate of return for this important role.

ACKNOWLEDGMENT

The research and preparation of *Six Myths in Modern Finance that Every Investor Needs to Know* has been a complex process spanning a period of six years. Along the way I have been helped and encouraged by many. Without their support, this book never would have been written or published.

In the beginning, three former Watson Wyatt Worldwide co-workers, Kjeld Sorensen, Jay Wolfe, and Herb Miller, helped significantly in gathering the necessary data to do the research. As the project evolved, they provided a careful review at every step of the way. They served as a sounding board for any new ideas, and provided candid feedback. At a critical step in the process, they provided the all-important financial support. But most importantly, it is their continued belief in the truth and importance of this effort that has served to keep the project going when it might otherwise have been abandoned. For this support, and their wonderful friendship, I am extremely grateful.

On the academic front, special thanks are offered to Dr. Allen Webster and the Board of Reviewers at the *Journal of Financial and Economic Practice*. First, they showed the foresight necessary to create a new journal, one that is dedicated to the publication of research which challenges conventional wisdom. Second, they provided editorial suggestions which significantly improved the three published research articles. Finally, they made the decision to actually publish articles which challenge some very core principles of modern finance. Given that these core principles have been long-standing and have received wide acclaim, the decision to publish the research articles could not have been easy. I am very thankful for their courage.

On the artistic front, a huge thank you is in order for Lindsey Craft. I first became acquainted with her artwork four years ago and when thinking of an artist to provide illustrations for this book, Lindsey was my first choice. She has been wonderful to work with throughout this entire process, and I could not be more pleased with the final illustrations. They are a significant enhancement to the book, and all credit for the ideas and execution goes to her.

Special thanks are also appropriate for Elliott Wolf of Classic Day Publishing. He offered valuable encouragement in the process, detailed technical suggestions, and provided the services of reviewers and technicians. At every step of the way Elliott either knew exactly what to do, or equally important, knew exactly who to do it. His selection of Cherie Tucker for technical review is a case in point. It is not an easy task to review a book about technical mathematical issues that is targeted for general readers. She took on the challenge with gusto, offering several hundred suggestions for changes in the text. All of her suggestions were adopted.

These last two paragraphs will be devoted to the all important contributions of family members. The first thank you goes to my sons, Jason and Brad. When I retired, they were very worried about what Dad would do to fill his time. This project has answered that question. But they have been much more that the usual support team offering the occasional "Go, Dad, Go," but have become active participants. Whenever either of them spotted a relevant article or heard an interesting newscast, he called it to my attention. This additional source of material, along with their cheerful encouragement, clearly helped to make this book a reality. Our discussions about how the project was progressing always helped to keep me grounded. For all this support, on top of being super sons, thank you, Jason and Brad.

Finally, the biggest thank you of all goes to my wife, Cheryl Haak. She has emotionally supported the project from the beginning. When my spirits would get low, her encouragement was instrumental. But she offered much more than the emotional support; she is the person who did all the typing! When you look at some of the mathematical formulas in the appendices, you will clearly see how thankful I am for her willingness to take on this challenge. But most importantly, she served in the role of target audience. She is not a mathematician or finance person, yet was willing to read every word of the text. If she did not see the point (which seemed 100% clear to me!), it was back to the drawing board for another rewrite. Her comments and suggestions, and the willingness to make them, help make this book much better than it ever would have been without her involvement. She is a fantastic partner in this project, but an even better partner in life.

Without the help of all the people listed above, the project would have never happened. I am thankful to each and every one for their contribution.

ABOUT THE AUTHOR

Mr. Joss is a retiree who enjoys recreational mathematics. Prior to retiring, Mr. Joss served as the chief technical actuary for the employee benefits consulting firm of Watson Wyatt Worldwide. In addition to being the author of many articles on pension plan design and funding, Mr. Joss is the author of three recently published papers dealing with mathematical issues in modern finance. All of his mathematics degrees (B.S. – 1968, M.A. – 1969, and Ph. D. – 1974) were received from the University of Washington. He and his wife, Cheryl, reside in Bellingham, Washington.